eating in

eating in

easy food for family and friends

THE AUSTRALIAN Women's Weekly

contents

Eating in has become one of today's great indulgences. At one time – and not so very long ago – that sentence would have read "eating OUT" but, given the hectic pace of life today, coming home to roost out on the patio with a pizza or to perch on the couch wielding chopsticks in one hand and a bowl of fried noodles in the other is sheer delight. For most of us, the comfort zone is the bottom line, and it becomes a five-star experience when shared with family and friends.

family food

barbecued pork fried rice

PREPARATION TIME 15 MINUTES **COOKING TIME** 30 MINUTES **SERVES** 6

3 cups (600g) long-grain rice

2 tablespoons peanut oil

2 teaspoons sesame oil

2 cloves garlic, crushed

3cm piece fresh ginger (15g), grated finely

1.125 litres (4½ cups) hot chicken stock

1 large brown onion (200g), sliced thinly

2 trimmed celery stalks (200g), sliced thinly

1 large carrot (180g), sliced thinly

6 green onions, sliced thickly

¼ cup (60ml) soy sauce

500g chinese barbecued pork

1 Rinse rice in a strainer under cold water until water runs clear.

2 Heat half of the peanut oil and half of the sesame oil in medium saucepan. Cook garlic and ginger until fragrant, add rice; toss rice to coat in garlic mixture. Add hot stock, bring to a boil. Reduce heat to low; cook, covered tightly, about 20 minutes or until rice is just tender. Do not remove lid or stir rice during cooking.

3 Heat remaining peanut oil and remaining sesame oil in wok; add brown onion, celery and carrot, stir-fry until softened. Add white part of green onion; stir-fry 1 minute. Add rice and sauce; stir-fry until combined. Serve topped with sliced pork and remaining green onion.

tip This recipe can be made several hours ahead; keep covered, in refrigerator. Chinese barbecued pork is available from Asian grocery stores.

per serving 22.4g total fat (7.3g saturated fat); 2796kJ (669 cal); 88.1g carbohydrate; 28.2g protein; 5.5g fibre

lamb patties with beetroot and tzatziki

PREPARATION TIME 20 MINUTES   **COOKING TIME** 10 MINUTES   **SERVES** 4

500g lamb mince

1 small brown onion (80g),
chopped finely

1 medium carrot (120g),
grated coarsely

1 egg, beaten lightly

1 clove garlic, crushed

2 tablespoons finely chopped
fresh flat-leaf parsley

1 teaspoon grated lemon rind

½ teaspoon dried oregano leaves

½ cup (140g) yogurt

1 clove garlic, crushed, extra

1 lebanese cucumber (130g),
seeded, chopped finely

1 tablespoon chopped fresh mint

1 large turkish bread (430g)

4 outer cos lettuce leaves, shredded

400g can whole baby beetroot,
drained, quartered

½ medium lemon (70g), quartered

1 Combine lamb, onion, carrot, egg, garlic, parsley, rind and oregano in large
   bowl; mix well. Shape mince mixture into eight patties.
2 Cook patties on heated, oiled grill plate (or barbecue), in batches, until
   browned and cooked through.
3 Meanwhile, combine yogurt, extra garlic, cucumber and mint in small bowl;
   mix well. Cut bread into four equal pieces, split each piece in half crossways;
   toast, cut-side up, until browned lightly.
4 Just before serving, sandwich bread equally with lettuce, patties, yogurt
   mixture and beetroot. Serve with lemon wedges.

tip The patties and yogurt mixture can be made several hours ahead; keep
covered, in refrigerator.

per serving 14.9g total fat (5.9g saturated fat); 2261kJ (541 cal);
61g carbohydrate; 40.1g protein; 7.2g fibre

fajitas and guacamole

PREPARATION TIME 15 MINUTES (PLUS REFRIGERATION TIME) **COOKING TIME** 20 MINUTES **SERVES** 4

Tex-mex cooking is responsible for spreading the popularity of fajitas among beef-lovers around the world. While the marinade can be made of a wide variety of ingredients, there are two requisites for any fajita recipe: it must always include capsicums of more than one colour and it should always be accompanied by guacamole.

600g piece beef scotch fillet
2 cloves garlic, crushed
¼ cup (60ml) lemon juice
1½ teaspoons ground cumin
½ teaspoon cayenne pepper
2 tablespoons olive oil
1 medium yellow capsicum (200g)
1 medium red capsicum (200g)
12 small flour tortillas
375g jar chunky salsa

GUACAMOLE
2 medium avocados (500g)
2 medium tomatoes (300g),
seeded, chopped finely
1 small red onion (100g),
chopped finely
2 tablespoons lime juice
2 tablespoons coarsely chopped
fresh coriander

1 Cut beef into thin 2cm-wide slices, place in medium bowl with garlic, juice, spices and oil; toss beef to coat in marinade. Cover; refrigerate 3 hours.

2 Quarter capsicums; discard seeds and membranes. Roast under grill or in very hot oven, skin-side up, until skin blisters and blackens. Cover capsicum pieces with plastic or paper for 5 minutes; peel away skin, then slice capsicums thinly.

3 Make guacamole.

4 Cook beef, in batches, on heated, oiled grill plate (or grill or barbecue) until browned and cooked as desired; cover to keep warm. Reheat capsicum strips on same heated grill plate.

5 Serve tortillas with beef, capsicum, guacamole and salsa.

GUACAMOLE Mash avocados roughly in medium bowl; add remaining ingredients, mix to combine.

tips Scotch fillet bought in a large piece is also known as rib-eye roast. You can also use rump for this recipe.

per serving 42.2g total fat (10g saturated fat); 2997kJ (717 cal); 42g carbohydrate; 42g protein; 6.5g fibre

beef and bean tacos

PREPARATION TIME 15 MINUTES **COOKING TIME** 20 MINUTES **MAKES** 8 TACOS

2 cloves garlic, crushed

150g lean beef mince

1 teaspoon chilli powder

½ teaspoon ground cumin

2 x 300g cans kidney beans, rinsed, drained

⅓ cup tomato paste

1 cup (250ml) water

2 medium tomatoes (300g), chopped coarsely

8 taco shells

½ small iceberg lettuce, shredded finely

SALSA CRUDA

1 lebanese cucumber (130g), seeded, chopped finely

1 small red onion (100g), chopped finely

2 small tomatoes (180g), seeded, chopped finely

2 teaspoons mild chilli sauce

1 Preheat oven to moderate (180°C/160°C fan-forced).

2 Heat large lightly oiled non-stick frying pan; cook garlic and beef, stirring, until beef is browned all over. Add chilli, cumin, beans, paste, the water and tomato; cook, covered, over low heat about 15 minutes or until mixture thickens slightly.

3 Meanwhile, place taco shells, upside-down, on oven tray; toast, uncovered, in moderate oven, 5 minutes.

4 Make salsa cruda.

5 Just before serving, fill taco shells with beef mixture, lettuce and salsa cruda.

SALSA CRUDA Combine ingredients in small bowl.

per taco 6g total fat (1.3g saturated fat); 736kJ (176 cal); 20g carbohydrate; 10.1g protein; 6.8g fibre

meat lovers' pizza

PREPARATION TIME 10 MINUTES **COOKING TIME** 25 MINUTES **SERVES** 4

2 teaspoons olive oil

1 small white onion (80g), chopped finely

1 clove garlic, crushed

250g beef mince

1 teaspoon paprika

⅓ cup (80ml) barbecue sauce

2 x 335g pizza bases (26cm round)

2 tablespoons tomato paste

2 cups (200g) pizza cheese

1 stick (125g) cabanossi, sliced coarsely

50g sliced spicy salami, chopped coarsely

1 Preheat oven to hot (220°C/200°C fan-forced).

2 Heat oil in medium non-stick frying pan; cook onion and garlic, stirring, until soft. Add beef; cook, stirring, until well browned. Stir in paprika and 1 tablespoon of the barbecue sauce. Remove from heat.

3 Place pizza bases on baking trays. Combine tomato paste with the remaining barbecue sauce and spread evenly over pizza bases. Sprinkle pizzas with half the cheese. Top with beef mixture, cabanossi, salami and remaining cheese.

4 Cook in hot oven about 15 minutes or until bases are crisp and topping is browned lightly. Serve with a green salad, if desired.

tips Pizza cheese is a pre-grated mix of mozzarella, cheddar and parmesan cheese.
Pizzas can be prepared several hours ahead; cook just before serving.

per serving 34.7g total fat (14.1g saturated fat); 3821kJ (914 cal); 100.7g carbohydrate; 49.6g protein; 7.3g fibre

steak sandwich revisited

PREPARATION TIME 20 MINUTES **COOKING TIME** 1 HOUR 20 MINUTES **SERVES** 4

4 beef scotch fillet steaks (800g)

8 thick slices crusty
white bread (360g)

2 tablespoons olive oil

60g rocket, trimmed

CHILLI TOMATO JAM

1 tablespoon olive oil

2 cloves garlic, crushed

4 medium tomatoes (600g),
chopped coarsely

1 tablespoon worcestershire sauce

½ cup (125ml) sweet chilli sauce

⅓ cup (75g) firmly packed
brown sugar

1 tablespoon coarsely chopped
fresh coriander

CARAMELISED LEEK

30g butter

1 medium leek (350g), sliced thinly

2 tablespoons brown sugar

2 tablespoons dry white wine

1 Make chilli tomato jam.

2 Make caramelised leek.

3 Cook beef on heated, oiled grill plate (or grill or barbecue) until browned and cooked as desired.

4 Meanwhile, brush both sides of bread slices with oil; toast both sides under hot grill. Sandwich rocket, beef, chilli tomato jam and caramelised leek between toast slices.

CHILLI TOMATO JAM Heat oil in medium saucepan; cook garlic, stirring, until browned lightly. Add tomato, sauces and sugar; bring to a boil. Reduce heat; simmer, uncovered, about 45 minutes or until mixture thickens. Stand 10 minutes; stir in coriander.

CARAMELISED LEEK Melt butter in medium frying pan; add leek, cook, stirring, until softened. Add sugar and wine; cook, stirring occasionally, about 20 minutes or until leek caramelises.

tips Chilli tomato jam can be made up to three days ahead; gently reheat when required.
We used a loaf of ciabatta for this recipe.

per serving 36.1g total fat (11.6g saturated fat); 3607kJ (863 cal); 80.5g carbohydrate; 53.6g protein; 8.9g fibre

minestrone

PREPARATION TIME 25 MINUTES **COOKING TIME** 15 MINUTES **SERVES** 4

1 tablespoon olive oil

1 small brown onion (80g), chopped finely

1 clove garlic, crushed

2 bacon rashers (140g), rind removed, chopped finely

1 trimmed celery stalk (100g), grated coarsely

2 medium carrots (240g), grated coarsely

410g can crushed tomatoes

2 cups (500ml) beef stock

1 litre (4 cups) water

½ cup (100g) short pasta

2 medium zucchini (240g), grated coarsely

300g can white beans, rinsed, drained

⅓ cup thinly sliced fresh basil

1 Heat oil in large saucepan; cook onion, garlic, bacon and celery, stirring, until vegetables just soften.

2 Add carrot, undrained tomato, stock, the water and pasta; bring to a boil. Reduce heat; simmer, covered, about 5 minutes or until pasta is just tender. Add zucchini and beans; bring to a boil. Remove from heat; stir in basil.

tips You can use any small pasta for this recipe, such as little shells, small macaroni or even risoni.
Many varieties of already-cooked white beans are available canned, including cannellini, butter and haricot beans; any of these are suitable for this soup.

per serving 6.4g total fat (1.1g saturated fat); 882kJ (211 cal); 26.2g carbohydrate; 12g protein; 7.8g fibre

chicken wings

honey soy wings

PREPARATION TIME 10 MINUTES
COOKING TIME 30 MINUTES **MAKES** 32

16 small chicken wings (1.3kg)
⅓ cup (120g) honey
½ cup (125ml) salt-reduced soy sauce
3 cloves garlic, crushed
4cm piece fresh ginger (20g), grated finely

1 Preheat oven to hot (220°C/200°C fan-forced).
2 Cut wings into three pieces at joints; discard tips.
   Combine chicken with remaining ingredients in
   large bowl; toss chicken to coat in soy mixture.
3 Place chicken, in single layer, in large shallow baking
   dish; brush any remaining soy mixture over chicken.
   Bake, uncovered, in hot oven, turning occasionally,
   about 30 minutes or until chicken is browned and
   cooked through. Serve with lemon wedges, if desired.

tip Wing tips can be used to make chicken stock.

per wing 1.4g total fat (0.4g saturated fat); 205kJ
(49 cal); 3.1g carbohydrate; 6.1g protein; 0.1g fibre

lime marmalade wings

PREPARATION TIME 20 MINUTES (PLUS REFRIGERATION TIME)
COOKING TIME 30 MINUTES **MAKES** 32

16 small chicken wings (1.3 kg)
¾ cup (250g) lime marmalade, warmed
½ cup (125ml) light soy sauce
⅓ cup (80ml) barbecue sauce
¼ cup (60ml) dry white wine
1 clove garlic, crushed
1 tablespoon lime juice

1 Preheat oven to hot (220°C/200°C fan-forced).
2 Cut wings into three pieces at joints; discard tips. Combine
   marmalade, sauces, wine and garlic in large bowl, add chicken;
   toss chicken to coat in marinade. Cover; refrigerate 3 hours
   or overnight.
3 Place chicken, in single layer, in large shallow baking dish; brush
   any remaining marinade over chicken. Bake, uncovered, in hot
   oven, turning occasionally, about 30 minutes or until chicken is
   browned and cooked through. Serve hot, drizzled with lime juice.

per wing 1.4g total fat (0.4g saturated fat); 259kJ
(62 cal); 6.2g carbohydrate; 6.1g protein; 0.1g fibre

tandoori wings

PREPARATION TIME 10 MINUTES (PLUS REFRIGERATION TIME)
COOKING TIME 30 MINUTES **MAKES** 32

16 small chicken wings (1.3kg)
½ cup (150g) tandoori paste
½ cup (140g) yogurt
1 medium brown onion (150g), grated

1 Preheat oven to hot (220°C/200°C fan-forced).
2 Cut wings into three pieces at joints; discard tips. Combine remaining ingredients in large bowl, add chicken; toss chicken to coat in mixture. Cover; refrigerate 3 hours or overnight.
3 Place chicken, in single layer, on oiled wire rack set inside large shallow baking dish. Roast, uncovered, in hot oven, about 30 minutes or until chicken is well browned and cooked through. Serve with lime wedges, if desired.

per wing 3g total fat (0.7g saturated fat); 234kJ (56 cal); 0.8g carbohydrate; 6.4g protein; 0.5g fibre

deep-south wings

PREPARATION TIME 10 MINUTES (PLUS REFRIGERATION TIME)
COOKING TIME 30 MINUTES **MAKES** 32

16 small chicken wings (1.3kg)
¼ cup (60ml) tomato sauce
¼ cup (60ml) worcestershire sauce
¼ cup (55g) brown sugar
1 tablespoon american mustard

DIPPING SAUCE
1 tablespoon american mustard
2 tablespoons tomato sauce
1 tablespoon worcestershire sauce
2 tablespoons brown sugar

1 Preheat oven to hot (220°C/200°C fan-forced).
2 Cut wings into three pieces at joints; discard tips. Combine chicken with remaining ingredients in large bowl. Cover; refrigerate 3 hours or overnight.
3 Place chicken, in single layer, on oiled wire rack set inside large shallow baking dish; brush remaining marinade over chicken. Roast, uncovered, in hot oven, about 30 minutes or until chicken is cooked through.

DIPPING SAUCE Combine ingredients in small bowl; cook, covered, in microwave oven on high (100%) for 1 minute. Serve with chicken wings.

per wing 1.4g total fat (0.4g saturated fat); 213kJ (51 cal); 38g carbohydrate; 6g protein; 0.1g fibre

stir-fried chicken and gai larn

PREPARATION TIME 10 MINUTES **COOKING TIME** 15 MINUTES **SERVES** 4

2 tablespoons sesame oil

500g chicken thigh fillets, sliced thinly

2 teaspoons sambal oelek

190g can sliced water chestnuts, drained

227g can bamboo shoot strips, drained

1 large red capsicum (350g), sliced thinly

⅓ cup (80ml) kecap manis

500g gai larn, chopped coarsely

2 cups (160g) bean sprouts

1 Heat half of the oil in wok; stir-fry chicken, in batches, until browned lightly.

2 Heat remaining oil in same wok; stir-fry sambal, chestnuts, bamboo and capsicum.

3 Return chicken to wok with kecap manis and gai larn; stir-fry until gai larn is just wilted and chicken is cooked through. Remove from heat; stir in sprouts.

tip Gai larn, also known as gai lum or chinese broccoli, can be found in Asian-food stores and many greengrocers.

per serving 18.9g total fat (4.1g saturated fat); 1338kJ (320 cal); 9g carbohydrate; 28.6g protein; 5.1g fibre

chilli beef stir-fry

PREPARATION TIME 10 MINUTES **COOKING TIME** 20 MINUTES **SERVES** 4

450g packet fresh hokkien noodles

¼ cup (60ml) peanut oil

700g piece beef rump steak,
sliced thinly

300g green beans, cut into
5cm lengths

1 clove garlic, chopped coarsely

2 fresh long red chillies, sliced

⅓ cup (100g) thai chilli jam
stir-fry paste

350g baby bok choy, quartered

¼ cup (60ml) beef stock

4 green onions, sliced thinly

⅓ cup firmly packed fresh
mint leaves

1 Place noodles in large heatproof bowl, cover with boiling water; separate noodles with fork. Drain.
2 Heat oil in wok; stir-fry beef, in batches, until browned all over.
3 Add beans to wok; stir-fry until almost tender. Add garlic, chilli and paste; stir-fry until fragrant. Add bok choy; stir-fry until just tender.
4 Return beef to wok with stock, noodles and onion. Stir-fry until hot; add mint, toss well.

tip This recipe is best made just before serving.

per serving 47.2g total fat (17.3g saturated fat); 3841kJ (919 cal); 70.3g carbohydrate; 53.2g protein; 12.8g fibre

breaded veal cutlets with
gnocchi in garlic mushroom sauce

PREPARATION TIME 15 MINUTES (PLUS REFRIGERATION TIME) **COOKING TIME** 30 MINUTES **SERVES** 4

2 eggs, beaten lightly

2 tablespoons milk

¼ cup (35g) plain flour

¾ cup (75g) packaged breadcrumbs

¾ cup (45g) stale breadcrumbs

¾ cup (80g) pizza cheese

½ cup coarsely chopped fresh
flat-leaf parsley

8 veal cutlets (1.3kg)

¼ cup (60ml) olive oil

2 cloves garlic, sliced thinly

250g mushrooms, sliced thinly

¾ cup (180ml) cream

½ cup (125ml) beef stock

625g packaged potato gnocchi

1 Whisk egg, milk and flour in medium bowl. Combine breadcrumbs, cheese and ⅓ cup of the parsley in another medium bowl. Coat cutlets, one at a time, in egg mixture then in cheese mixture. Place cutlets, in single layer, on tray. Cover; refrigerate 10 minutes.

2 Heat half of the oil in large frying pan; cook cutlets, in batches, until browned both sides and cooked as desired. Cover to keep warm.

3 Heat remaining oil in same pan; cook garlic and mushroom, stirring, until mushroom is soft. Add cream and stock; bring to a boil. Reduce heat; simmer, stirring, until sauce thickens slightly.

4 Meanwhile, cook gnocchi in large saucepan of boiling water, uncovered, until gnocchi float to the surface. Remove from pan with slotted spoon; place in large bowl.

5 Stir remaining parsley into sauce; pour sauce over gnocchi, toss to combine.

6 Serve gnocchi with cutlets and steamed green beans, if desired.

per serving 46.3g total fat (20.2g saturated fat); 4172kJ (998 cal); 75.5g carbohydrate; 69.5g protein; 7.3g fibre

hearty lamb and barley soup

PREPARATION TIME 40 MINUTES (PLUS REFRIGERATION TIME) **COOKING TIME** 2 HOURS 50 MINUTES **SERVES** 6

2 tablespoons olive oil

2 small carrots (140g),
chopped finely

2 trimmed celery stalks (200g),
chopped finely

2 cloves garlic, crushed

¾ cup (150g) pearl barley

3 sprigs fresh oregano

½ cup coarsely chopped fresh
flat-leaf parsley

1 tablespoon lemon juice,
approximately

LAMB STOCK

2 tablespoons olive oil

1.2kg lamb neck chops

3 medium brown onions (450g),
chopped coarsely, skins left on

2 medium carrots (240g),
chopped coarsely

2 trimmed celery stalks (200g),
chopped coarsely

2 bay leaves

1 teaspoon black peppercorns

8 stalks fresh flat-leaf parsley

2 sprigs fresh thyme

4 litres (16 cups) water

1 Make lamb stock.
2 Pull meat off bones; reserve meat, discard bones.
3 Heat oil in large, clean saucepan; add carrot, celery and garlic, cook, stirring, until softened. Add barley; stir to coat in mixture.
4 Add oregano and prepared lamb stock; bring to a boil. Reduce heat, simmer, covered, about 30 minutes or until barley is tender. Blend or process one-third of the soup until smooth. Return processed soup to pan.
5 Add reserved lamb meat; simmer, covered, about 5 minutes or until meat is hot.
6 Just before serving, stir in parsley and juice to taste.

LAMB STOCK Heat half of the oil in large saucepan. Add lamb; cook, in batches, until well browned. Heat remaining oil in same pan, add vegetables; cook, stirring, until well browned. Return lamb to pan with remaining ingredients. Bring to a boil, then reduce heat, skim surface; simmer, uncovered, 2 hours, skimming surface occasionally. Strain stock through muslin-lined strainer into large, clean bowl, reserving lamb neck chops; discard vegetables. Refrigerate stock for several hours or overnight, then discard solidified fat from stock surface.

tip The lamb stock can be made up to two days ahead.

per serving 31.4g total fat (10.2g saturated fat); 2119kJ (507 cal); 23.2g carbohydrate; 33.3g protein; 7.2g fibre

creamy pumpkin and sage ravioli

PREPARATION TIME 15 MINUTES **COOKING TIME** 25 MINUTES **SERVES** 6

¼ cup (60ml) olive oil

16 fresh sage leaves

½ large butternut pumpkin (900g),
peeled, sliced

1 medium leek (350g),
chopped finely

1 tablespoon shredded fresh
sage leaves, extra

1 tablespoon white balsamic
condiment

300ml cream

900g fresh or frozen ricotta ravioli

1 Heat 2 tablespoons of the oil in large frying pan, fry sage leaves until bright green; remove with slotted spoon or tongs, drain on absorbent paper.

2 Heat remaining oil in same pan; add pumpkin, cook in batches until browned on both sides and just tender. Turn pumpkin carefully to prevent it breaking; cover to keep warm.

3 Add leek to frying pan; cook, stirring, about 5 minutes or until softened.

4 Add shredded extra sage, balsamic and cream; bring to a boil then simmer, uncovered, until sauce has thickened slightly.

5 Meanwhile, cook pasta in large saucepan of boiling water, uncovered, until just tender; drain.

6 Combine drained pasta with pumpkin and cream mixture; serve topped with fried sage leaves.

tips This recipe is best made close to serving.
White balsamic condiment is slightly sweet, and is available
in the vinegar section in supermarkets.

per serving 38.9g total fat (18.8g saturated fat); 2241kJ (536 cal);
32g carbohydrate; 15.5g protein; 4.9g fibre

pork larb

PREPARATION TIME 20 MINUTES **COOKING TIME** 20 MINUTES **SERVES** 4

1 tablespoon peanut oil

2 tablespoons finely chopped fresh lemon grass

2 fresh small red thai chillies, chopped finely

2 cloves garlic, crushed

8cm piece fresh ginger (40g), grated finely

1.5kg pork mince

2 tablespoons fish sauce

⅔ cup (160ml) lime juice

5 fresh kaffir lime leaves, shredded finely

⅔ cup loosely packed fresh mint leaves

½ cup loosely packed fresh coriander leaves

4 green onions, sliced thinly

4 shallots (100g), sliced thinly

8 large iceberg lettuce leaves

pot wok pan

1 Heat oil in large non-stick frying pan; cook lemon grass, chilli, garlic and ginger, stirring, until fragrant. Add pork; cook, stirring, until cooked through. Add sauce and half of the juice; cook, stirring, 5 minutes. Transfer mixture to large bowl; stir in lime leaves, herbs, onion, shallot and remaining juice.

2 Place two lettuce leaves together to form a "bowl" on each serving plate; divide larb among leaves.

tip Larb is a classic thai salad that can be made with beef, chicken or pork mince, or vegetables.

per serving 29.5g total fat (10g saturated fat); 2408kJ (576 cal); 3.6g carbohydrate; 72.9g protein; 3.5g fibre

warm salmon, risoni and pea salad

PREPARATION TIME 15 MINUTES **COOKING TIME** 15 MINUTES **SERVES** 4

250g risoni pasta
2 cups (250g) frozen peas
1 tablespoon olive oil
500g salmon fillets
8 green onions, chopped
100g baby spinach leaves

DILL DRESSING
¼ cup (60ml) olive oil
2 teaspoons grated lemon rind
¼ cup (60ml) lemon juice
½ teaspoon white sugar
1 teaspoon dijon mustard
1 tablespoon coarsely chopped
fresh dill

1 Make dill dressing.
2 Cook pasta in large saucepan of boiling water until almost tender. Add peas to pan with pasta and cook until peas and pasta are just tender; drain. Transfer to a large bowl.
3 Meanwhile, heat oil in large non-stick frying pan. Add salmon; cook until browned lightly and cooked as desired. Remove from pan; stand 5 minutes. Remove skin and any bones; break salmon into large chunks.
4 Add onion, spinach and dill dressing to pasta; toss well. Add salmon, toss gently to combine.

DILL DRESSING Combine ingredients in screw-top jar; shake well.

tip This recipe can be made three hours ahead and served cold.

per serving 28.2g total fat (4.7g saturated fat); 2508kJ (600 cal); 49.9g carbohydrate; 36.1g protein; 6.9g fibre

warm potato and smoked chicken salad

PREPARATION TIME 20 MINUTES **COOKING TIME** 15 MINUTES **SERVES** 4

700g kipfler potatoes

500g frozen broad beans

500g smoked chicken breasts, sliced thinly

1 large red onion (300g), sliced thinly

100g rocket

2 tablespoons drained baby capers, rinsed

PARSLEY DRESSING

½ cup firmly packed fresh flat-leaf parsley leaves

⅓ cup (80ml) olive oil

2 tablespoons lemon juice

1 clove garlic, crushed

1 teaspoon dijon mustard

1 Boil or steam potatoes and beans, separately, until tender.
2 Meanwhile, make parsley dressing.
3 Combine remaining ingredients in large bowl.
4 Cut hot potatoes into thin wedges; peel beans. Add potato, beans
   and parsley dressing to salad; toss gently to combine.

PARSLEY DRESSING Blend or process parsley and oil until chopped finely.
Transfer to small bowl; whisk in juice, garlic and mustard.

tips Use a sturdy brush to scrub the potatoes well before cooking. Some
kitchenware stores stock brushes especially designed for cleaning potatoes.
You can use thin slices of cooked chicken as a substitute for the smoked
chicken, if preferred.
This recipe can be prepared several hours ahead.

per serving 246g total fat (4.2g saturated fat); 1956kJ (468 cal);
29.4g carbohydrate; 31.4g protein; 10g fibre

mushroom and rocket risotto

PREPARATION TIME 10 MINUTES **COOKING TIME** 35 MINUTES **SERVES** 4

2 cups (500ml) chicken stock

3½ cups (875ml) water

50g butter

2 tablespoons olive oil

250g button mushrooms, sliced thickly

2 cloves garlic, crushed

2 medium brown onions (300g), sliced thinly

2 cups (400g) arborio rice

¼ cup chopped fresh flat-leaf parsley

¾ cup (60g) grated parmesan cheese

30g butter, chopped, extra

250g rocket, trimmed

1 Combine stock and the water in large saucepan; bring to a boil then reduce heat to simmer gently.

2 Meanwhile, heat half of the butter and half of the oil in another large saucepan; add mushroom, cook, stirring, until browned lightly. Add garlic; cook, stirring, until fragrant. Remove from pan; cover to keep warm.

3 Heat remaining butter and remaining oil in same pan; cook onion, stirring, until soft. Add rice, stir over medium heat until rice is coated in butter mixture. Stir in ½ cup (125ml) of the stock mixture; cook, stirring, over low heat until liquid is absorbed.

4 Continue adding stock mixture, in ½-cup batches, stirring after each addition until liquid is absorbed. The total cooking time should be about 20 minutes or until rice is tender.

5 Stir in mushroom mixture, parsley, cheese, extra butter and rocket. Top with extra parmesan cheese flakes, if desired.

tip This recipe is best made close to serving.

per serving 93.6g total fat (56g saturated fat); 5229kJ (1251 cal); 85.9g carbohydrate; 19.3g protein; 6.2g fibre

roast pork with pears and parsnips

PREPARATION TIME 15 MINUTES **COOKING TIME** 55 MINUTES **SERVES** 6

6-cutlet pork rib roast (1kg),
french-trimmed, rind scored, tied

2 teaspoons olive oil

1 tablespoon sea salt

2 small red onions (200g), quartered

2 medium parsnips (500g), quartered

3 small Packham pears (540g),
cored, quartered

4 cloves garlic, unpeeled

¼ cup (55g) brown sugar

2 tablespoons olive oil, extra

1 Preheat oven to very hot (240°C/220°C fan-forced).

2 Rub pork rind with oil and salt. Place pork on wire rack in baking dish.

3 In separate baking dish, gently combine remaining ingredients.

4 Bake pork and pear mixture in very hot oven about 25 minutes or until pork rind blisters; reduce temperature to moderate (180°C/160°C fan-forced). Cook in moderate oven further 25 minutes or until pork is cooked through. Turn or shake pear mixture occasionally.

5 Remove pork and vegetables from oven, cover with foil; stand pork about 10 minutes before cutting.

6 Serve pork with pear mixture.

tips This recipe is best made close to serving.
Ask your butcher to score the rind of the pork for you.

per serving 22.8g total fat (5.3g saturated fat); 1810kJ (433 cal);
26g carbohydrate; 31.8g protein; 5.9g fibre

vegetable and fetta freeform tarts

PREPARATION TIME 30 MINUTES (PLUS STANDING TIME) COOKING TIME 50 MINUTES SERVES 4

1 small eggplant (230g),
chopped coarsely

coarse cooking salt

1 tablespoon olive oil

1 medium brown onion (150g),
sliced thinly

2 medium zucchini (240g),
sliced thinly

4 sheets ready-rolled
shortcrust pastry

¼ cup (65g) bottled pesto

120g fetta cheese, crumbled

8 cherry tomatoes, halved

1 tablespoon finely chopped
fresh basil

1 egg, beaten lightly

1 Place eggplant in sieve or colander; sprinkle all over with salt, then stand sieve over sink or large bowl for 15 minutes. Rinse eggplant well under cold running water, drain; pat dry with absorbent paper.

2 Preheat oven to moderate (180°C/160°C fan-forced).

3 Heat oil in large non-stick frying pan; cook onion, stirring, until softened. Add eggplant and zucchini to pan; cook, stirring, until vegetables are softened.

4 Using a plate as a guide, cut a 20cm round from each pastry sheet; place rounds on oven trays. Spread equal amounts of pesto in centre of each round, leaving a 4cm border around the outside edge.

5 Divide vegetables among rounds over pesto; top each with equal amounts of cheese, tomato and basil. Using hands, turn the 4cm edge on each round over filling; brush around pastry edge with egg.

6 Bake, uncovered, in moderate oven about 40 minutes or until pastry is browned lightly.

tip Allowing the eggplant to stand a while covered with salt will help withdraw most of the vegetable's slightly bitter juice; it also helps prevent the eggplant from absorbing too much oil when it's cooked. Be sure to rinse the eggplant well under cold running water to remove as much of the salt as possible, and to dry it thoroughly with absorbent paper before cooking.

per serving 57.6g total fat (27.4g saturated fat); 3578kJ (856 cal); 65.2g carbohydrate; 19.9g protein; 5.7g fibre

pepper-roasted garlic and lemon chicken

PREPARATION TIME 35 MINUTES **COOKING TIME** 1 HOUR 50 MINUTES **SERVES** 4

2 bulbs garlic

2kg chicken

cooking-oil spray

2 teaspoons salt

2 tablespoons cracked black pepper

1 medium lemon (140g),
cut into 8 wedges

1 cup (250ml) water

3 medium globe artichokes (600g)

2 tablespoons lemon juice

2 medium red onions (340g),
quartered

3 baby fennel bulbs (390g),
trimmed, halved

2 medium leeks (700g), halved
lengthways then quartered

250g cherry tomatoes

⅓ cup (80ml) dry white wine

¼ cup (60ml) lemon juice, extra

1 Preheat oven to moderately hot (200°C/180°C fan-forced).

2 Separate cloves from garlic bulb, leaving skin intact. Wash chicken under cold water; pat dry inside and out with absorbent paper. Coat chicken with cooking-oil spray; press combined salt and pepper onto skin and inside cavity. Place garlic and lemon inside cavity; tie legs together with kitchen string. Place chicken on small wire rack in large flameproof baking dish, pour the water in baking dish; roast, uncovered, in moderately hot oven 50 minutes.

3 Meanwhile, discard outer leaves from artichokes; cut tips from remaining leaves. Trim then peel stalks. Quarter artichokes lengthways; using teaspoon remove chokes. Cover artichoke with cold water in medium bowl, stir in the 2 tablespoons of lemon juice; soak artichoke until ready to cook.

4 Add drained artichoke, onion, fennel and leek to dish with chicken; coat with cooking-oil spray. Roast, uncovered, in moderately hot oven about 40 minutes or until vegetables are just tender.

5 Add tomatoes to dish; roast, uncovered, in moderately hot oven about 20 minutes or until tomatoes soften and chicken is cooked through. Place chicken on serving dish and vegetables in large bowl; cover to keep warm.

6 Stir wine and extra juice into dish with pan juices; bring to a boil. Boil 2 minutes then strain sauce over vegetables; toss gently to combine.

7 Discard garlic and lemon from cavity; serve chicken with vegetables.

per serving 35.7g total fat (10.7g saturated fat); 2771kJ (663 cal); 18.8g carbohydrate; 62g protein; 14.6g fibre

New York steaks with lemon thyme butter

PREPARATION TIME 15 MINUTES (PLUS REFRIGERATION TIME) **COOKING TIME** 45 MINUTES **SERVES** 4

4 large potatoes (1.2kg),
cut into wedges

2 medium red onions (340g),
cut into wedges

1 medium lemon (140g),
cut into wedges

2 teaspoons fresh thyme leaves

¼ cup (60ml) olive oil

4 New York-cut beef steaks (880g)

LEMON THYME BUTTER

60g butter, softened

2 teaspoons finely grated
lemon rind

1 teaspoon finely chopped
fresh thyme

1 clove garlic, crushed

1 Preheat oven to hot (220°C/200°C fan-forced).

2 Make lemon thyme butter.

3 Combine potato, onion, lemon, thyme and oil in large deep baking dish. Bake, uncovered, in hot oven, stirring occasionally, about 45 minutes or until potato is browned and crisp.

4 Meanwhile, cook beef, in batches, on heated, oiled grill plate (or grill or barbecue) until browned both sides and cooked as desired.

5 Serve beef with potato and onion mixture, topped with lemon thyme butter.

LEMON THYME BUTTER Combine ingredients in small bowl. Cover; refrigerate until firm.

tip New York-cut steaks are also known as boneless sirloin steaks.

per serving 46.4g total fat (19.1g saturated fat); 3306kJ (791 cal); 38.6g carbohydrate; 53.6g protein; 6.3g fibre

fish and spring onion pies

PREPARATION TIME 20 MINUTES **COOKING TIME** 40 MINUTES **SERVES** 4

4 medium spring onions

40g butter

1 medium carrot (120g), chopped finely

2 trimmed celery stalks (200g), chopped finely

2 tablespoons plain flour

1 cup (250ml) fish stock

½ cup (125ml) cream

1 tablespoon lemon juice

1 teaspoon dijon mustard

750g boneless white fish fillets, chopped coarsely

1 tablespoon chopped fresh dill

1 tablespoon chopped fresh chives

1 egg, beaten lightly

1 sheet ready-rolled butter puff pastry, cut into quarters

1 Trim onions, leaving about 6cm of the stems. Cut one onion into four slices lengthways; reserve. Chop remaining onions coarsely.

2 Melt butter in large saucepan; add remaining onion with carrot and celery. Cook, stirring, until vegetables soften.

3 Add flour to saucepan; cook, stirring, 1 minute. Add stock and cream; cook, stirring, until sauce boils and thickens. Stir in lemon juice and mustard.

4 Add fish to pan, stir gently. Cover, simmer until fish is just cooked. Gently stir in herbs.

5 Preheat oven to moderately hot (200°C/180°C fan-forced).

6 Spoon mixture into four 1-cup (250ml) ovenproof dishes; place on oven tray. Brush dish edges with egg, top with pastry; trim. Brush pastry with more egg and top with reserved onion.

7 Bake in moderately hot oven about 25 minutes or until pastry is puffed and browned lightly.

per serving 43.6g total fat (25.9g saturated fat); 3051kJ (730 cal); 38.7g carbohydrate; 46.1g protein; 3.3g fibre

barbecued sweet and sour blue-eye

PREPARATION TIME 20 MINUTES **COOKING TIME** 20 MINUTES **SERVES** 4

1 small pineapple (900g),
chopped coarsely

1 large red capsicum (350g),
chopped coarsely

1 medium green capsicum (200g),
chopped coarsely

1 medium red onion (170g),
sliced thinly

4 blue-eye fillets (800g)

2 tablespoons caster sugar

½ cup (125ml) white vinegar

2 tablespoons soy sauce

1 fresh long red chilli, sliced thinly

4cm piece fresh ginger (20g),
grated finely

3 green onions, sliced thinly

1 Cook pineapple, capsicums and red onion on heated, lightly oiled grill plate (or grill or barbecue) until browned all over and tender.

2 Meanwhile, cook fish on heated, lightly oiled flat plate (or large non-stick frying pan) until cooked as desired.

3 Combine sugar, vinegar, soy, chilli and ginger in large bowl. Place pineapple, capsicums and red onion in bowl with dressing; toss gently to combine. Divide mixture among serving plates; top with fish and green onion.

per serving 6g total fat (2.2g saturated fat); 1434kJ (343 cal); 24.9g carbohydrate; 46g protein; 4.6g fibre

lamb cutlets with char-grilled vegetable salad

PREPARATION TIME 10 MINUTES **COOKING TIME** 15 MINUTES **SERVES** 4

⅓ cup (80ml) olive oil

350g kumara, sliced thinly

2 tablespoons balsamic vinegar

1 clove garlic, crushed

12 french-trimmed
lamb cutlets (600g)

150g marinated char-grilled
eggplant, sliced thickly

150g marinated char-grilled
capsicum, sliced thickly

125g char-grilled artichokes,
quartered, optional

2 cups loosely packed fresh
flat-leaf parsley leaves

2 tablespoons lemon juice

1 Combine one tablespoon of the oil with kumara in medium bowl. Cook kumara on heated, oiled barbecue (or grill plate or frying pan) until browned lightly and cooked through.

2 Combine another tablespoon of the oil with vinegar and garlic in small bowl; brush over lamb. Cook lamb on heated, oiled barbecue (or grill plate or frying pan) until browned lightly and cooked as desired.

3 In large bowl, toss kumara with eggplant, capsicum, artichokes and parsley. Drizzle with combined juice and remaining oil. Serve lamb with vegetable mixture.

tip This recipe is best made close to serving.

per serving 49.4g total fat (12.8g saturated fat); 2533kJ (606 cal); 14.6g carbohydrate; 26.2g protein; 2.7g fibre

asparagus, bacon and parmesan tortiglioni

PREPARATION TIME 15 MINUTES **COOKING TIME** 25 MINUTES **SERVES** 4

500g tortiglioni pasta

500g asparagus, chopped coarsely

2 teaspoons olive oil

5 bacon rashers (350g),
sliced thinly

1 clove garlic, crushed

100g butter, chopped

¼ cup coarsely chopped fresh
flat-leaf parsley

½ cup (40g) grated parmesan cheese

½ cup (50g) grated mozzarella cheese

1 Cook pasta in large saucepan of boiling water, uncovered, until just tender. Drain; return to pan.

2 Meanwhile, boil, steam or microwave asparagus until just tender; drain.

3 Heat oil in large frying pan; add bacon, cook, stirring, until crisp. Add garlic, cook until fragrant.

4 Add bacon mixture to drained pasta with butter, asparagus, parsley and a quarter of the combined cheeses; toss gently.

5 Preheat grill to hot. Transfer pasta mixture to shallow 2.5 litre (10-cup) ovenproof dish. Sprinkle top of pasta with remaining cheese, grill until browned lightly.

per serving 32g total fat (18.3g saturated fat); 3219kJ (770 cal); 87.7g carbohydrate; 32.5g protein; 5.7g fibre

moroccan chicken with couscous

PREPARATION TIME 10 MINUTES **COOKING TIME** 10 MINUTES **SERVES** 4

4 single chicken breast fillets (680g)

⅓ cup (80ml) moroccan marinade

2 cups (500ml) vegetable stock

2 cups (400g) couscous

20g butter

1 small red onion (100g), sliced thinly

2 fresh small red thai chillies, seeded, chopped finely

½ cup (110g) coarsely chopped seeded prunes

⅓ cup (45g) slivered almonds, toasted

½ cup coarsely chopped fresh mint

¼ cup (50g) finely chopped preserved lemon

1 Toss chicken in large bowl with marinade; stand 10 minutes. Cook chicken, in batches, on heated, oiled grill plate (or grill or barbecue) until browned lightly and cooked through. Stand 5 minutes; slice chicken thickly.

2 Meanwhile, bring stock to a boil in medium saucepan. Remove from heat; stir in couscous and butter. Cover; stand 5 minutes or until liquid is absorbed, fluffing couscous with fork occasionally. Stir in remaining ingredients. Serve chicken on couscous.

tips Preserved lemons are available from specialty shops and delicatessens. Rinse well under cold water, discard flesh, then finely chop the rind. Moroccan marinade is a bottled blend of garlic, capsicum, chilli, lemon and various spices, and can be found at your local supermarket.

per serving 16.2g total fat (4.6g saturated fat); 3097kJ (741 cal); 91.5g carbohydrate; 56g protein; 5.1g fibre

chicken caesar salad

PREPARATION TIME 20 MINUTES **COOKING TIME** 35 MINUTES **SERVES** 4

1 long french bread stick

⅓ cup (80ml) olive oil

2 cloves garlic, crushed

600g chicken breast fillets

4 bacon rashers (280g),
rind removed

1 large cos lettuce, trimmed, torn

6 green onions, sliced thinly

¼ cup coarsely chopped fresh
flat-leaf parsley

100g parmesan cheese, shaved

CAESAR DRESSING

1 egg

1 clove garlic, quartered

2 tablespoons lemon juice

1 teaspoon dijon mustard

6 anchovy fillets, drained

⅔ cup (160ml) olive oil

1 tablespoon hot water,
approximately

1 Preheat oven to moderate (180°C/160°C fan-forced).

2 Make caesar dressing.

3 Halve bread lengthways; slice halves on the diagonal into 1cm-thick slices. Combine oil and garlic in large bowl, add bread; toss bread to coat in mixture. Place bread, in single layer, on oven trays; toast in moderate oven about 10 minutes or until croûtes are browned lightly.

4 Meanwhile, cook chicken, in batches, on heated, oiled grill plate (or grill or barbecue) until browned lightly and cooked through. Cook bacon on same grill plate until browned and crisp; drain on absorbent paper. Slice chicken thinly; slice bacon thinly.

5 Combine half the chicken, half the bacon, half the croûtes and half the dressing in large bowl with lettuce and half the onion, half the parsley and half the cheese; toss gently.

6 Divide salad among serving bowls; top with remaining chicken, bacon, croûtes, onion, parsley and cheese, drizzle with remaining dressing.

CAESAR DRESSING Blend or process egg, garlic, juice, mustard and anchovies until smooth. With motor operating, add oil in a thin, steady stream until dressing thickens. If thinner dressing is preferred, stir in as much of the water as desired.

tip Caesar dressing and croûtes can be prepared a day ahead. Cover and refrigerate dressing; store croûtes in airtight container.

per serving 76.5g total fat (16.5g saturated fat); 4661kJ (1115 cal); 44.1g carbohydrate; 64g protein; 8.3g fibre

chocolate banana bread

PREPARATION TIME 15 MINUTES **COOKING TIME** 1 HOUR **SERVES** 12

1 cup mashed banana

¾ cup (165g) caster sugar

2 eggs, beaten lightly

¼ cup (60ml) extra light olive oil

¼ cup (60ml) milk

⅔ cup (100g) self-raising flour

⅔ cup (100g) wholemeal
self-raising flour

¾ cup (90g) coarsely chopped
toasted walnuts

¼ cup (45g) finely chopped
dark eating chocolate

WHIPPED NUT BUTTER

100g butter, softened

¼ cup (30g) finely chopped
toasted walnuts

1 Preheat oven to moderate (180°C/160°C fan-forced). Grease 14cm x 21cm loaf pan; line base and long sides with baking paper.

2 Combine banana and sugar in large bowl; stir in egg, oil and milk. Add remaining ingredients; stir until combined.

3 Spread mixture into prepared pan; bake, uncovered, in moderate oven about 1 hour. Stand bread in pan 5 minutes; turn onto wire rack, cool 5 minutes.

4 Meanwhile, make whipped nut butter.

5 Serve bread warm with whipped nut butter.

WHIPPED NUT BUTTER Beat butter in small bowl with electric mixer until light and fluffy; stir in nuts.

tips You need about two large overripe bananas (460g) for this recipe. Leftover banana bread can be toasted, if desired.

per serving 20.7g total fat (6.7g saturated fat); 1392kJ (333 cal); 32.8g carbohydrate; 5.2g protein; 2.5g fibre

mango and raspberry jelly

PREPARATION TIME 20 MINUTES (PLUS REFRIGERATION TIME) **SERVES** 8

425g can sliced mango
85g packet mango jelly crystals
2 cups (500ml) boiling water
150g raspberries
85g packet raspberry jelly crystals
1 cup (250ml) cold water
300ml thickened cream

1 Drain mango in sieve over small bowl; reserve liquid. Measure ¼ cup mango slices and reserve. Divide remaining mango slices among eight ¾-cup (180ml) glasses.

2 Combine mango jelly crystals with 1 cup of the boiling water in small bowl, stirring until jelly dissolves. Add enough cold water to reserved mango liquid to make 1 cup of liquid; stir into mango jelly. Divide evenly among glasses over mango, cover; refrigerate about 2 hours or until jelly sets.

3 Divide raspberries among glasses over jelly. Combine raspberry jelly crystals and remaining cup of the boiling water in small bowl, stirring until jelly dissolves; stir in the cold water. Divide evenly among glasses over raspberries, cover; refrigerate about 2 hours or until jelly sets.

4 Beat cream in small bowl with electric mixer until soft peaks form. Spread cream equally among glasses; top with reserved mango.

tip If mangoes are in season, you can use one large fresh mango weighing about 600g for this recipe. Peel the mango over a small bowl to catch as much of the juice as possible, then cut off mango cheeks; slice cheeks thinly. Squeeze as much juice as possible from around the mango seed into bowl with other juice; add enough cold water to make 1 cup of liquid to be added to the mango jelly crystals (see step 2).

per serving 13.9g total fat (9.1g saturated fat); 1003kJ (240 cal); 26.7g carbohydrate; 2.9g protein; 1.5g fibre

apricot muesli slice

PREPARATION TIME 25 MINUTES **COOKING TIME** 30 MINUTES (PLUS COOLING TIME) **MAKES** ABOUT 20 SLICES

100g butter, softened
½ cup (110g) caster sugar
1 egg yolk
⅔ cup (100g) plain flour
¼ cup (35g) self-raising flour
1 tablespoon custard powder
½ cup (160g) apricot jam, warmed

MUESLI TOPPING
¼ cup (90g) honey
50g butter
1½ cups (135g) rolled oats
1 cup (40g) cornflakes
½ cup (35g) shredded coconut
½ cup (75g) finely chopped
dried apricots

1 Preheat oven to moderate (180°C/160°C fan-forced). Grease 20cm x 30cm lamington pan; line base with baking paper, extending paper 5cm over edges of long sides of pan.

2 Beat butter, sugar and yolk in small bowl with electric mixer until light and fluffy. Stir in sifted combined flours and custard powder. Using fingers, press mixture over base of prepared pan. Bake, uncovered, in moderate oven about 15 minutes or until browned lightly.

3 Meanwhile, make muesli topping.

4 Remove slice from oven, spread with jam. Sprinkle muesli topping over jam, pressing gently with fingers. Return to oven; bake another 15 minutes. Cool slice in pan. Cut into 20 pieces to serve.

MUESLI TOPPING Heat honey and butter in small saucepan until butter melts; transfer to large bowl. Stir in remaining ingredients.

per slice 8.3g total fat (5.3g saturated fat); 790kJ (189 cal); 27.5g carbohydrate; 2.1g protein; 1.5g fibre

mixed berry buttermilk muffins

PREPARATION TIME 5 MINUTES **COOKING TIME** 20 MINUTES **MAKES** 12

2½ cups (375g) self-raising flour
¾ cup (165g) caster sugar
1 egg, beaten lightly
1 teaspoon vanilla extract
⅔ cup (160ml) vegetable oil
¾ cup (180ml) buttermilk
200g frozen mixed berries

1 Preheat oven to moderately hot (200°C/180°C fan-forced). Lightly grease 12-hole (⅓-cup/80ml) muffin pan or ovenproof dishes.

2 Sift dry ingredients into large bowl, stir in remaining ingredients; do not overmix. Spoon mixture into prepared pan. Bake in moderately hot oven about 20 minutes. Turn muffins onto wire rack to cool.

tips Use still-frozen berries to minimise "bleeding" of colour into the mixture. We used 100g frozen raspberries, 50g frozen blueberries and 50g frozen blackberries in this recipe.

per muffin 13.4g total fat (1.9g saturated fat); 1191kJ (285 cal); 37.1g carbohydrate; 4.6g protein; 1.6g fibre

tropical fruit salad

PREPARATION TIME 20 MINUTES **COOKING TIME** 15 MINUTES (PLUS COOLING AND REFRIGERATION TIME) **SERVES** 6

2 cups (500ml) water

⅓ cup (90g) grated palm sugar

2cm piece fresh ginger (10g), chopped finely

2 star anise

2 tablespoons lime juice

¼ cup coarsely chopped fresh mint

2 large mangoes (1.2kg), diced into 2cm pieces

1 small honeydew melon (1.3kg), diced into 2cm pieces

1 small pineapple (900g), chopped coarsely

2 medium oranges (480g), segmented

¼ cup (60ml) passionfruit pulp

12 fresh lychees (300g), peeled, seeded, halved

1 Stir the water and sugar in small saucepan over heat, without boiling, until sugar dissolves; bring to a boil. Boil, uncovered, without stirring, 5 minutes. Add ginger and star anise; simmer, uncovered, about 5 minutes or until syrup thickens slightly. Discard star anise; cool to room temperature. Stir in juice and mint.

2 Place prepared fruit in large bowl with syrup; toss gently to combine. Refrigerate until cold.

tip You need three passionfruit for this recipe.

per serving 0.8g total fat (0g saturated fat); 828kJ (198 cal); 42.8g carbohydrate; 4.3g protein; 7.9g fibre

refrigerator cookies

PREPARATION TIME 20 MINUTES (PLUS REFRIGERATION TIME) **COOKING TIME** 10 MINUTES **MAKES** 50

250g butter, softened
1 cup (160g) icing sugar mixture
2½ cups (375g) plain flour

1 Beat butter and sifted icing sugar in small bowl with electric mixer until light and fluffy. Transfer to large bowl.
2 Stir flour, in two batches, into butter mixture. Knead dough on lightly floured surface until smooth. Divide dough in half; roll each half into a 25cm log. Enclose in plastic wrap; refrigerate about 1 hour or until firm.
3 Meanwhile, preheat oven to moderate (180°C/160°C fan-forced).
4 Cut rolls into 1cm slices; place on greased oven trays 2cm apart. Bake, uncovered, in moderate oven about 10 minutes or until browned lightly. Turn cookies onto wire racks to cool.

per cookie 4.2g total fat (2.7g saturated fat); 314kJ (75 cal); 8.6g carbohydrate; 0.8g protein; 0.3g fibre

variations

VANILLA

Beat 1 teaspoon vanilla extract into butter and sugar mixture.

per cookie 4.2g total fat (2.7g saturated fat); 314kJ (75 cal); 8.6g carbohydrate; 0.8g protein; 0.3g fibre

CHOCOLATE AND HAZELNUT

Beat 2 tablespoons sifted cocoa powder into butter and sugar mixture, then stir in ⅓ cup (35g) hazelnut meal and ¼ cup (45g) finely chopped milk chocolate Bits before adding the flour. Bring back to room temperature before slicing.

per cookie 4.8g total fat (2.9g saturated fat); 347kJ (83 cal); 9.3g carbohydrate; 1.1g protein; 0.4g fibre

LEMON

Beat 1 teaspoon finely grated lemon rind into butter and sugar mixture.

per cookie 4.2g total fat (2.7g saturated fat); 314kJ (75 cal); 8.6g carbohydrate; 0.8g protein; 0.3g fibre

ORANGE

Beat 1 teaspoon finely grated orange rind into butter and sugar mixture.

per cookie 4.2g total fat (2.7g saturated fat); 314kJ (75 cal); 8.6g carbohydrate; 0.8g protein; 0.3g fibre

tips The thinner the slice, the crisper the cookie.
Keep this dough, rolled into a log shape and tightly sealed in plastic wrap, in your fridge for up to three days or in your freezer for up to three months. The frozen dough should be defrosted in the refrigerator before slicing and baking.

apricot almond crumbles

PREPARATION TIME 15 MINUTES **COOKING TIME** 30 MINUTES **SERVES** 6

825g can apricot halves in
natural juice
1 tablespoon brandy
½ cup (75g) self-raising flour
¾ teaspoon ground ginger
¼ cup (30g) ground almonds
¼ cup (55g) brown sugar
¼ cup (55g) caster sugar
90g butter, chopped

1 Preheat oven to moderate (180°C/160°C fan-forced).

2 Drain apricots over a small jug or bowl; reserve ½ cup (125ml) juice.

3 Slice apricots and divide among six ¾-cup (180ml) ovenproof dishes; place dishes on oven tray. Combine brandy with reserved juice; pour over apricots.

4 Sift flour and ginger into medium bowl; stir in almonds and sugars, then rub in butter with fingertips.

5 Sprinkle crumble mixture over fruit and bake in moderate oven about 30 minutes or until browned lightly. Serve hot with ice-cream or cream, if desired.

tip This recipe is best made close to serving.

per serving 15.2g total fat (8.3g saturated fat); 1304kJ (312 cal); 39.6g carbohydrate; 3.4g protein; 3.5g fibre

lemon tartlets

PREPARATION TIME 40 MINUTES (PLUS REFRIGERATION TIME)
COOKING TIME 30 MINUTES (PLUS COOLING TIME) **MAKES** 12

1 sheet ready-rolled
butter puff pastry
20g butter, melted
1 teaspoon caster sugar
2 tablespoons icing sugar mixture
1 egg, separated
⅓ cup (75g) caster sugar, extra
10g butter melted, extra
⅓ cup (80ml) milk
1 teaspoon finely grated lemon rind
1½ tablespoons lemon juice
2 tablespoons self-raising flour

1 Cut pastry sheet in half; stand on a board for 5 minutes or until partially thawed. Liberally grease a 12-hole, deep patty pan with a pastry brush dipped in the melted butter. Cut 12 x 10cm squares of baking paper.

2 Sprinkle half of pastry with caster sugar, top with remaining pastry half. Roll pastry stack up tightly from the short side. Refrigerate until firm.

3 Cut pastry log into 12 x 1cm-wide pieces. Place one pastry piece, spiral-side down, on board dusted with sifted icing sugar mixture; refrigerate remaining pastry. Roll out pastry piece into a 10cm round. Cut a round from the pastry using a 9cm cutter. Press the round into a patty pan hole. Repeat with the remaining pastry pieces. Freeze for 10 minutes.

4 Preheat oven to hot (220°C/200°C fan-forced).

5 Place baking paper squares over pastry in pan; place about a tablespoon of dried rice or beans over paper. Bake 10 minutes in hot oven; remove paper and rice. Reduce temperature to moderately slow (160°C/140°C fan-forced), bake further 10 minutes in moderately slow oven or until base of pastry is browned lightly and crisp. Cool.

6 Reduce oven temperature to slow (140°C/120°C fan-forced).

7 Meanwhile, beat egg yolk and 2 tablespoons of extra sugar in small bowl with electric mixer until thick and creamy; fold in extra butter, milk, rind and juice, then sifted flour.

8 Beat egg white in small, clean bowl with electric mixer until soft peaks form. Gradually add remaining extra sugar; beat until sugar dissolved. Fold into lemon mixture in two batches; divide among pastry cases.

9 Bake in slow oven about 10 minutes or until just set. Remove tartlets from pan; cool on wire rack.

10 Serve tartlets dusted with sifted icing sugar, if desired.

tip This recipe is best made on the day of serving.

per tartlet 18.2g total fat (11.5g saturated fat); 966kJ (231 cal); 15.7g carbohydrate; 1.9g protein; 0.3g fibre

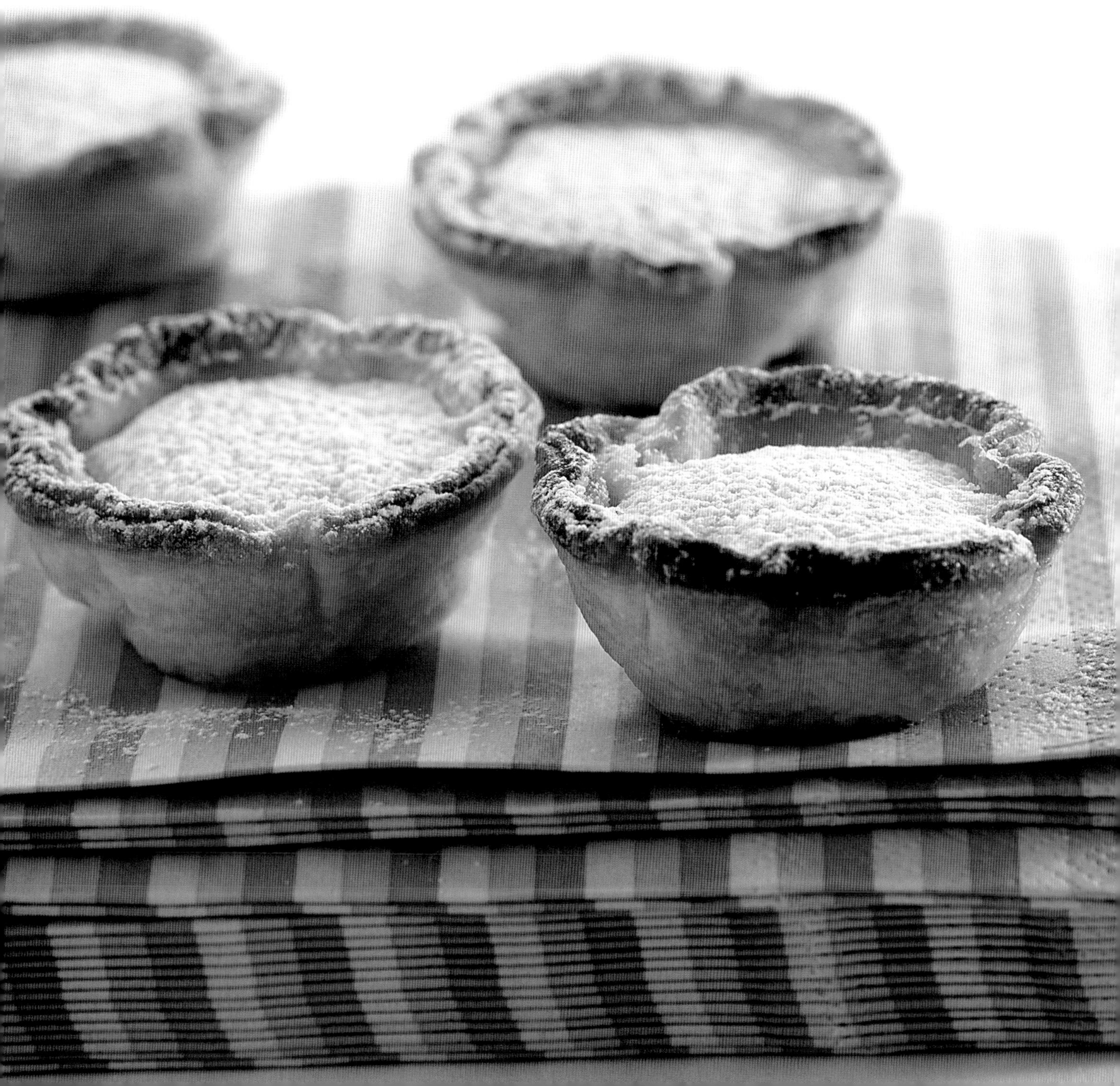

pecan and chocolate brownies

PREPARATION TIME 15 MINUTES **COOKING TIME** 25 MINUTES **MAKES** 8

80g butter, chopped

150g dark eating chocolate, chopped

¾ cup (165g) firmly packed brown sugar

2 eggs, beaten lightly

1 teaspoon vanilla extract

⅔ cup (100g) plain flour

1 tablespoon cocoa powder

50g dark eating chocolate, chopped, extra

¼ cup (30g) chopped pecans

1 Preheat oven to moderately hot (200°C/180°C fan-forced). Grease eight holes of a 12-hole (⅓-cup/80ml) muffin pan; line bases with rounds of baking paper.

2 Combine butter, chocolate and sugar in medium heavy-based saucepan; stir over low heat until smooth.

3 Transfer mixture to large bowl; stir in egg, extract, sifted flour and cocoa, then extra chocolate. Divide mixture among holes of prepared pan. Sprinkle with nuts; bake in moderately hot oven about 20 minutes. Stand muffins in pan for a few minutes before turning onto wire rack to cool.

tip Brownies can be made three days ahead; store in an airtight container.

per brownie 19.6g total fat (10.3g saturated fat); 1509kJ (361 cal); 43.3g carbohydrate; 4.9g protein; 1.1g fibre

steamed jam puddings

PREPARATION TIME 15 MINUTES **COOKING TIME** 25 MINUTES **SERVES** 4

⅓ cup (110g) raspberry jam
1 egg
½ cup (110g) caster sugar
1 cup (150g) self-raising flour
½ cup (125ml) milk
25g butter, melted
1 tablespoon boiling water
1 teaspoon vanilla extract

1 Preheat oven to moderate (180°C/160°C fan-forced). Grease four ¾-cup (180ml) metal moulds; divide jam among moulds.

2 Beat egg and sugar in small bowl with electric mixer until thick and creamy. Fold in sifted flour and milk, in two batches, then combined butter, water and extract.

3 Top jam with pudding mixture. Place moulds in medium baking dish; pour enough boiling water into dish to come halfway up sides of moulds. Bake, uncovered, about 25 minutes. Stand 5 minutes; turn onto serving plates. Serve puddings warm with vanilla custard or cream, if desired.

tip You can use any flavour of jam for this recipe.

per serving 8.1g total fat (4.7g saturated fat); 1622kJ (388 cal); 74g carbohydrate; 6.5g protein; 1.9g fibre

cooking for friends

smoked seafood and mixed vegetable antipasti
PREPARATION TIME 35 MINUTES SERVES 4

⅓ cup (80g) sour cream

2 teaspoons raspberry vinegar

1 tablespoon coarsely chopped
fresh chives

1 clove garlic, crushed

1 large yellow zucchini (150g)

1 tablespoon raspberry vinegar, extra

¼ cup (60ml) extra virgin olive oil

⅓ cup (45g) slivered almonds,
toasted

1 cup (150g) drained
semi-dried tomatoes

1 large avocado (320g)

1 tablespoon lemon juice

300g hot-smoked ocean trout
portions

200g sliced smoked salmon

16 drained caperberries (80g)

1 large lemon (180g),
cut into wedges

170g packet roasted garlic
bagel crisps

1 Combine sour cream, vinegar, chives and garlic in small bowl, cover; refrigerate until required.

2 Meanwhile, using vegetable peeler, slice zucchini lengthways into ribbons; combine zucchini in small bowl with extra vinegar and 2 tablespoons of the oil.

3 Combine nuts, tomatoes and remaining oil in small bowl.

4 Slice avocado thickly into small bowl; sprinkle with juice.

5 Flake trout into bite-sized pieces.

6 Arrange zucchini mixture, nut mixture, avocado, trout, salmon and caperberries on large platter; serve with sour cream mixture, lemon wedges and bagel crisps.

tip Hot-smoked trout is available at most supermarkets in filleted portions of various sizes; we used two 150g portions for this recipe.

per serving 54.8g total fat (12.7g saturated fat); 3624kJ (867 cal); 48.5g carbohydrate; 44.5g protein; 8.8g fibre

duck in crisp wonton cups

PREPARATION TIME 20 MINUTES **COOKING TIME** 20 MINUTES (PLUS COOLING TIME) **MAKES** 24

24 wonton wrappers
cooking-oil spray
1 chinese barbecued duck
1 tablespoon hoisin sauce
1 tablespoon soy sauce
2 tablespoons coarsely chopped
fresh coriander
2 green onions, chopped coarsely
2 green onions, extra, sliced thinly

1 Preheat oven to moderate (180°C/160°C fan-forced). Grease 24 mini (1½-tablespoons/30ml) muffin pans.

2 Press wonton wrappers into pans to form a cup shape; spray lightly with oil. Bake in moderate oven about 8 minutes until browned lightly. Remove from muffin pans, cool.

3 Remove flesh and skin from duck, slice thinly, discard fat. Place duck on oven tray, cover with foil, heat in moderate oven for 10 minutes.

4 Combine duck with sauces, coriander and chopped onions in medium bowl.

5 Spoon duck mixture into wonton cups, top with sliced onions.

tips Wonton cups can be made a day ahead; store in an airtight container. The filling can be prepared several hours ahead. Assemble close to serving. Chinese barbecued duck is available from Asian grocery stores.

per cup 13.5g total fat (3.9g saturated fat); 732kJ (175 cal); 3.6g carbohydrate; 10g protein; 0.3g fibre

vietnamese rice paper rolls

PREPARATION TIME 50 MINUTES **COOKING TIME** 15 MINUTES **MAKES** 24

1 tablespoon peanut oil

2 chicken breast fillets (340g)

24 x 17cm-square rice paper sheets

1 small red capsicum (150g),
sliced thinly

1¼ cups (100g) bean sprouts

1 cup firmly packed fresh
mint leaves

1 cup firmly packed fresh
coriander leaves

DIPPING SAUCE

1 clove garlic, crushed

2 tablespoons fish sauce

¼ cup (60ml) lime juice

¼ cup (60ml) oyster sauce

¼ cup (65g) finely grated
palm sugar

2 fresh small red thai chillies,
chopped finely

1 Make dipping sauce.

2 Heat oil in small frying pan; cook chicken until browned all over and cooked through. Stand 10 minutes; slice thinly into 24 pieces.

3 Place one sheet of rice paper in medium bowl of warm water until just softened; carefully lift from water. Place on board; pat dry with absorbent paper. Position rice paper in diamond shape; place chicken slice vertically down centre of rice paper, top with capsicum, sprouts, mint and coriander. Fold bottom corner over filling; roll rice paper from side to side to enclose filling. Repeat with remaining rice paper sheets and filling.

4 Serve rice paper rolls cold with dipping sauce.

DIPPING SAUCE Combine ingredients in small saucepan; stir over medium heat until sugar dissolves. Refrigerate until cold.

tips Chicken can be cooked a day ahead. Cover, refrigerate until required. Dipping sauce can be made a day ahead. Cover, refrigerate until required.

per roll 1.2g total fat (0.3g saturated fat); 159kJ (38 cal); 2.7g carbohydrate; 3.9g protein; 0.6g fibre
per tablespoon dipping sauce 0.1g total fat (0g saturated fat); 121kJ (29 cal); 6.7g carbohydrate; 0.5g protein; 0.1g fibre

zucchini fritters with tzatziki

PREPARATION TIME 20 MINUTES (PLUS REFRIGERATION AND STANDING TIME) **COOKING TIME** 20 MINUTES **MAKES** 24

4 medium zucchini (480g), grated coarsely

1 teaspoon salt

1 medium brown onion (150g), chopped finely

¾ cup (45g) stale breadcrumbs

2 eggs, beaten lightly

1 tablespoon finely chopped fresh oregano

1 tablespoon finely chopped fresh mint

2 tablespoons extra virgin olive oil

TZATZIKI

2 cups (560g) thick Greek-style yogurt

1 lebanese cucumber (130g)

1 clove garlic, crushed

2 tablespoons finely chopped fresh mint

2 tablespoons lemon juice

1　Make tzatziki.
2　Combine zucchini and salt. Stand 15 minutes, then squeeze out excess liquid. Combine zucchini with onion, breadcrumbs, egg, oregano and mint.
3　Preheat oven to very slow (120°C/100°C fan-forced).
4　Heat oil in non-stick frying pan over medium heat; drop in tablespoonfuls of zucchini mixture, flatten slightly; cook until browned lightly both sides and cooked through. Transfer to oven tray; place in very slow oven to keep warm. Repeat with remaining mixture.
5　Serve fritters with tzatziki.

TZATZIKI　Line a sieve with absorbent paper. Add yogurt, place over a bowl. Cover, refrigerate at least 4 hours. Halve cucumber lengthways; remove seeds. Coarsely grate flesh and skin. Squeeze out excess liquid. Combine yogurt, cucumber, garlic, mint and juice in medium bowl.

tip　Fritters can be made several hours ahead.

per fritter　3.3g total fat (1.4g saturated fat); 242kJ (58 cal); 4.4g carbohydrate; 2.5g protein; 0.7g fibre

deep-fried prawn balls

PREPARATION TIME 25 MINUTES (PLUS REFRIGERATION TIME) **COOKING TIME** 10 MINUTES **SERVES** 4

1kg cooked large prawns

5 green onions, chopped finely

2 cloves garlic, crushed

4 fresh small red thai chillies, chopped finely

1cm piece fresh ginger (5g), grated finely

1 tablespoon cornflour

2 teaspoons fish sauce

¼ cup coarsely chopped fresh coriander

¼ cup (25g) packaged breadcrumbs

½ cup (35g) stale breadcrumbs

vegetable oil, for deep-frying

⅓ cup (80ml) sweet chilli sauce

1 lime (60g), cut into wedges

1 Shell and devein prawns; cut in half. Blend or process prawn, pulsing, until chopped coarsely. Place in large bowl with onion, garlic, chilli, ginger, cornflour, fish sauce and coriander; mix well.

2 Using hands, roll rounded tablespoons of prawn mixture into balls. Roll prawn balls in combined breadcrumbs; place, in single layer, on plastic-wrap-lined tray. Cover, refrigerate 30 minutes.

3 Heat oil in wok; deep-fry prawn balls, in batches, until browned lightly. Serve with sweet chilli sauce and lime wedges.

tips Dip your fingers in cold water when shaping the prawn balls to prevent the mixture from sticking to them.
Placing prawn balls on a plastic-wrap-lined tray and refrigerating them for at least half an hour before frying will firm them and help ensure they don't fall apart during cooking.
Prawn balls can be shaped a day ahead and kept, covered, in the refrigerator.

per serving 10.7g total fat (1.5g saturated fat); 1175kJ (281 cal); 17.3g carbohydrate; 28.5g protein; 2.4g fibre

dips

chile con queso

PREPARATION TIME 10 MINUTES
COOKING TIME 10 MINUTES
MAKES 2 CUPS

2 teaspoons vegetable oil
½ small green capsicum (75g), chopped finely
½ small brown onion (40g), chopped finely
1 tablespoon drained bottled jalapeño chillies, chopped finely
1 clove garlic, crushed
½ x 400g can undrained chopped peeled tomatoes
250g packet cream cheese, softened

1 Heat oil in medium saucepan; cook capsicum, onion, chilli and garlic, stirring, until onion softens. Add tomato; cook, stirring, 2 minutes.
2 Remove from heat. Add cheese; whisk until cheese melts and dip is smooth.
3 Serve warm with crispy corn chips, if desired.

per tablespoon 3.9g total fat (2.3g saturated fat); 171kJ (41 cal); 0.7g carbohydrate; 1g protein; 0.2g fibre

butter bean dip with pitta crisps

PREPARATION TIME 10 MINUTES
COOKING TIME 8 MINUTES
MAKES 1 CUP

1 clove garlic, crushed
¼ cup lightly packed fresh flat-leaf parsley leaves
400g can butter beans, rinsed, drained
1 teaspoon ground cumin
⅓ cup (80ml) olive oil
6 pitta bread (400g), cut into sixths

1 Preheat oven to moderately hot (200°C/180°C fan-forced).
2 Blend or process garlic, parsley, beans and cumin until combined. With motor operating, add the oil in a thin stream until mixture is smooth.
3 Place pitta pieces on lightly greased oven trays; bake in moderately hot oven 8 minutes or until browned lightly.
4 Serve dip with pitta crisps.

tips This recipe can be made a day ahead. Store pitta crisps in an airtight container.

per tablespoon 5.5g total fat (0.8g saturated fat); 493kJ (118 cal); 14.3g carbohydrate; 2.9g protein; 1.2g fibre

turkish spinach dip

PREPARATION TIME 10 MINUTES
COOKING TIME 10 MINUTES
(PLUS COOLING AND REFRIGERATION TIME)
MAKES 2 CUPS

1 tablespoon olive oil
1 small brown onion (80g), chopped finely
1 clove garlic, crushed
1 teaspoon ground cumin
½ teaspoon curry powder
¼ teaspoon ground turmeric
100g trimmed spinach leaves, shredded finely
500g thick Greek-style yogurt

1 Heat oil in medium frying pan; cook onion and garlic, stirring, until onion softens. Add spices; cook, stirring, until fragrant. Add spinach; cook, stirring, until spinach wilts. Transfer mixture to serving bowl; cool.
2 Stir yogurt through mixture, cover; refrigerate 1 hour.
3 Serve cold with toasted turkish bread, if desired.

tips You need a bunch of spinach weighing 300g for this recipe. Dip can be made a day ahead. Cover; refrigerate until required.

per tablespoon 2.2g total fat (1.1g saturated fat); 142kJ (34 cal); 2.1g carbohydrate; 1.3g protein; 0.2g fibre

guacamole

PREPARATION TIME 10 MINUTES
MAKES 2½ CUPS

3 medium avocados (750g), peeled, chopped
½ small red onion (50g), chopped finely
1 large egg tomato (90g), seeded, chopped finely
1 tablespoon lime juice
¼ cup coarsely chopped fresh coriander

1 Mash avocado in medium bowl; stir in remaining ingredients.

per tablespoon 4g total fat (0.9g saturated fat); 159kJ (38 cal); 0.2g carbohydrate; 0.4g protein; 0.3g fibre

eggs with pancetta

PREPARATION TIME 15 MINUTES **COOKING TIME** 20 MINUTES **SERVES** 4

2 teaspoons olive oil

1 small red capsicum (150g), chopped finely

6 slices pancetta (90g), chopped finely

100g mushrooms, chopped finely

4 green onions, chopped finely

⅓ cup (25g) finely grated parmesan cheese

8 eggs

2 teaspoons coarsely chopped fresh flat-leaf parsley

1 Preheat oven to moderately hot (200°C/180°C fan-forced). Lightly oil four ¾-cup (180ml) ovenproof dishes.

2 Heat oil in medium frying pan; cook capsicum and pancetta, stirring, until capsicum is just tender. Add mushroom and onion; cook, stirring, until onion just softens. Remove from heat; stir in half the cheese.

3 Divide capsicum mixture among dishes; break two eggs into each dish. Bake, uncovered, in moderately hot oven 5 minutes. Sprinkle remaining cheese over eggs; bake further 5 minutes or until eggs are just set. Sprinkle with parsley just before serving.

per serving 18g total fat (6g saturated fat); 1074kJ (257 cal); 2.5g carbohydrate; 21.6g protein; 1.2g fibre

asparagus and gruyere tart

PREPARATION TIME 25 MINUTES (PLUS REFRIGERATION AND FREEZING TIME)
COOKING TIME 55 MINUTES (PLUS COOLING TIME) **SERVES** 4

25g butter

1 small white onion (80g),
sliced thinly

12 asparagus spears, halved
crossways

2 eggs

1 teaspoon plain flour

¾ cup (180ml) cream

50g gruyere cheese, grated coarsely

PASTRY

¾ cup (110g) plain flour

75g butter

1 tablespoon finely grated
parmesan cheese

pinch of paprika

1 egg yolk

2 teaspoons iced water

1 Make pastry.

2 Increase oven temperature to moderately hot (200°C/180°C fan-forced).

3 Heat butter in large frying pan; cook onion over low heat without browning, about 10 minutes or until very soft.

4 Meanwhile, add asparagus to small saucepan of boiling water, cook 1 minute; drain. Place into bowl of iced water; drain.

5 Whisk eggs, flour and cream in medium jug.

6 Place onion in pastry base, top with asparagus and cheese. Place tart on an oven tray, gently pour egg mixture over asparagus; carefully place tart in oven.

7 Bake in moderately hot oven about 20 minutes or until browned lightly and set.

PASTRY Process flour, butter, parmesan and paprika until crumbly. Add yolk and iced water; pulse until mixture just comes together. Knead pastry on lightly floured surface until smooth. Wrap pastry in plastic wrap; refrigerate 30 minutes. Roll pastry until large enough to line 10cm x 34cm rectangular loose-base flan tin. Lift pastry into tin, ease into sides, trim edges. Freeze 30 minutes. Preheat oven to moderate (180°C/160°C fan-forced). Cover pastry with baking paper, fill with dried beans or rice, place on oven tray. Bake in moderate oven 15 minutes, remove paper and beans or rice, bake further 10 minutes; cool.

tip This recipe is best made on the day of serving.

per serving 48.9g total fat (30.5g saturated fat); 2445kJ (585 cal); 23.6g carbohydrate; 14.2g protein; 2.3g fibre

roasted vegetable and haloumi salad

PREPARATION TIME 15 MINUTES **COOKING TIME** 45 MINUTES **SERVES** 4

1 medium kumara (400g),
chopped coarsely

2 large carrots (360g),
quartered lengthways

2 medium parsnips (500g),
halved lengthways

2 cloves garlic, crushed

¼ cup (60ml) extra virgin olive oil

2 large red onions (600g),
cut into wedges

4 baby eggplants (240g),
halved lengthways

4 fresh long red chillies, halved

250g haloumi cheese, sliced

75g baby spinach leaves

LEMON AND BASIL DRESSING

½ cup (125ml) extra virgin olive oil

2 tablespoons lemon juice

¼ cup coarsely chopped fresh basil

1 teaspoon white sugar

1 Preheat oven to hot (220°C/200°C fan-forced).

2 Combine kumara, carrot, parsnip and half the combined garlic and olive oil on large shallow oven tray. Combine onion, eggplant, chilli and remaining oil mixture on separate shallow oven tray. Roast kumara mixture in hot oven about 45 minutes and onion mixture about 30 minutes, or until vegetables are cooked and browned lightly.

3 Meanwhile, make lemon and basil dressing.

4 Just before serving, heat lightly oiled grill plate; cook cheese until browned lightly on both sides.

5 Combine roasted vegetables with spinach; divide among serving plates. Top with cheese and drizzle with lemon and basil dressing.

LEMON AND BASIL DRESSING Blend or process ingredients until smooth.

tip Lemon and basil dressing can be made several hours ahead.

per serving 53.6g total fat (12.8g saturated fat); 2880kJ (689 cal); 33g carbohydrate; 20.3g protein; 9.8g fibre

char-grilled prawns with mango chilli salsa

PREPARATION TIME 15 MINUTES **COOKING TIME** 5 MINUTES **SERVES** 4

1kg uncooked large prawns

MANGO CHILLI SALSA

¼ cup (60ml) lime juice

2 fresh small red thai chillies, chopped finely

¼ cup (60ml) olive oil

2 teaspoons fish sauce

2 teaspoons grated palm sugar

1 medium mango (430g), chopped

1 medium green mango (430g), sliced thinly

1 small red onion (100g), sliced thinly

½ cup firmly packed fresh coriander leaves

1 Make mango chilli salsa.

2 Cook prawns in their shells on heated, oiled grill plate (or grill or barbecue) until changed colour and cooked through.

3 Serve prawns with mango chilli salsa.

MANGO CHILLI SALSA Combine juice, chilli, oil, sauce and sugar in medium bowl; stir until the sugar is dissolved. Add mangoes, onion and coriander; toss gently.

tips Salsa can be prepared three hours ahead.
Palm sugar can be substituted with brown sugar.

per serving 14.8g total fat (2.1g saturated fat); 1405kJ (336 cal); 22.5g carbohydrate; 27.9g protein; 3g fibre

mushroom, capsicum and cheese omelettes

PREPARATION TIME 15 MINUTES **COOKING TIME** 15 MINUTES **SERVES** 4

20g butter

1 small red capsicum (150g),
sliced thinly

200g mushrooms, sliced thinly

2 tablespoons finely chopped
fresh chives

8 eggs

1 tablespoon milk

4 green onions, sliced thinly

½ cup (60g) coarsely grated
cheddar cheese

1 Melt butter in large frying pan; cook capsicum, mushroom and chives,
  stirring occasionally, until vegetables soften. Drain vegetable filling on
  absorbent-paper-lined plate; cover with foil to keep warm.

2 Whisk eggs until well combined, then whisk in milk and onion.

3 Pour half the egg mixture into same pan used for the vegetables; tilt
  pan to cover base with egg mixture. Cook over medium heat about
  4 minutes or until omelette is just set.

4 Carefully spoon half the vegetable filling onto one half of the omelette;
  sprinkle half the cheese over vegetable filling. Use a spatula to lift and
  fold unfilled omelette half over vegetable filling. Carefully slide omelette
  onto plate; cover with foil to keep warm.

5 Make one more omelette with remaining egg mixture, vegetable filling and
  cheese. Cut each omelette in half; place one half on each serving plate.

tips Vegetable filling can be prepared up to a day ahead. Reheat gently
over low heat when required.
Omelettes are best made at time of serving.
We used button mushrooms for our omelettes, but you can choose any
variety you like.

per serving 19.7g total fat (8.7g saturated fat); 1087kJ (260 cal);
3.2g carbohydrate; 19.2g protein; 1.9g fibre

thai chicken and lychee salad

PREPARATION TIME 20 MINUTES **SERVES** 4

3 cups (480g) shredded
cooked chicken

565g can lychees in syrup,
drained, halved

1 small red onion (100g),
sliced thinly

8 green onions, sliced thinly

2 cups (160g) bean sprouts

½ cup firmly packed fresh
mint leaves

½ cup firmly packed fresh
coriander leaves

1 teaspoon finely grated lime rind

1 teaspoon sambal oelek

¼ cup (60ml) lime juice

1 teaspoon sesame oil

1 tablespoon brown sugar

2 teaspoons fish sauce

1 Combine chicken, lychees, onions, sprouts, mint and coriander in large bowl.
2 Combine remaining ingredients in screw-top jar; shake well. Drizzle dressing over salad; toss gently to combine.

tip You need to buy a barbecued chicken weighing about 900g for this recipe.

per serving 7.6g total fat (1.9g saturated fat); 1112kJ (266 cal); 28g carbohydrate; 21.8g protein; 4.4g fibre

strawberry hotcakes with blueberry sauce

PREPARATION TIME 15 MINUTES **COOKING TIME** 20 MINUTES **SERVES** 4

1 egg, separated
½ cup (125ml) apple sauce
1 teaspoon vanilla extract
2 cups (560g) low-fat yogurt
1¾ cups (260g) wholemeal
self-raising flour
250g strawberries, hulled,
chopped coarsely
2 egg whites, extra

BLUEBERRY SAUCE
150g blueberries, chopped coarsely
2 tablespoons white sugar
1 tablespoon water

1 Make blueberry sauce.

2 Combine egg yolk, apple sauce, extract, yogurt, flour and strawberries in large bowl.

3 Using electric mixer, beat all egg whites in small bowl until soft peaks form. Fold egg whites into yogurt mixture.

4 Pour ¼-cup batter into heated large lightly greased non-stick frying pan; using spatula, spread batter to shape into a round. Cook, over low heat, until bubbles appear on the surface. Turn hotcake; cook until browned lightly on other side. Remove from pan; cover to keep warm. Repeat with remaining batter. Serve with blueberry sauce.

BLUEBERRY SAUCE Combine ingredients in small saucepan; bring to a boil, stirring constantly. Reduce heat; simmer 2 minutes. Remove from heat; cool. Blend or process blueberry mixture until smooth.

per serving 3.2g total fat (0.8g saturated fat); 1735kJ (415 cal); 73.4g carbohydrate; 21.5g protein; 10.3g fibre

turkish-style pizza with minted yogurt
PREPARATION TIME 15 MINUTES **COOKING TIME** 35 MINUTES **SERVES** 6

1 tablespoon olive oil

1 medium brown onion (150g), chopped finely

1 clove garlic, crushed

500g beef or lamb mince

¼ teaspoon cayenne pepper

2 teaspoons ground cumin

½ teaspoon ground cinnamon

1½ teaspoons mixed spice

1 teaspoon grated lemon rind

2 tablespoons lemon juice

1 cup (250ml) beef stock

2 medium tomatoes (300g), chopped finely

⅓ cup (50g) pine nuts, toasted

¼ cup finely chopped fresh parsley

¼ cup finely chopped fresh mint

2 x 430g turkish bread

200g yogurt

1 tablespoon finely chopped fresh mint, extra

1 Preheat oven to hot (220°C/200°C fan-forced).

2 Heat oil in large frying pan, add onion and garlic; cook, stirring, until onion is soft. Add mince; cook until browned. Add pepper and spices; stir until fragrant.

3 Add rind, juice, stock and tomatoes to pan; cook, stirring over medium heat until most of the liquid is evaporated. Remove from heat, stir in pine nuts and chopped herbs.

4 Place bread on oven trays; press mince mixture evenly over top of bread leaving 3cm border.

5 Cover pizzas with foil; bake in hot oven 10 minutes. Remove foil; bake further 10 minutes until browned lightly.

6 Cut into thick slices; serve topped with combined yogurt and extra chopped mint.

tips Pizza is best baked just before serving.
Mince mixture can be made a day ahead.

per serving 21.9g total fat (5.5g saturated fat); 2767kJ (662 cal); 78.9g carbohydrate; 35.5g protein; 6g fibre

smoked salmon on rösti

PREPARATION TIME 20 MINUTES **COOKING TIME** 20 MINUTES **SERVES** 4

4 medium potatoes (800g)

2 tablespoons vegetable oil

½ cup (120g) spreadable light cream cheese

1 tablespoon finely chopped fresh flat-leaf parsley

1 tablespoon finely chopped fresh chives

1 tablespoon lemon juice

150g sliced smoked salmon

1 Coarsely grate peeled potatoes; use hands to squeeze out as much excess liquid as possible. Measure ¼ cups of grated potato, placing each portion on long sheet of baking paper.

2 Heat 2 teaspoons of the oil in large non-stick frying pan; place two portions of the grated potato in pan, flattening each with a spatula. Cook rösti over medium heat until browned; turn with spatula to cook other side. Drain rösti on absorbent paper; make six more rösti with remaining oil and grated potato.

3 Combine cream cheese, herbs and juice in small bowl.

4 Divide rösti among serving plates, top with herbed cream cheese and smoked salmon.

tip Rösti are Swiss pan-fried potato cakes, and are best made from a "starchy" potato variety, such as spunta or russet burbank.

per serving 16.1g total fat (4.8g saturated fat); 1275kJ (305 cal); 24.2g carbohydrate; 15.4g protein; 2.9g fibre

cold seafood platter with dipping sauces

PREPARATION TIME 1 HOUR (PLUS STANDING TIME) **SERVES** 4

1 cooked large lobster (1.2kg)
2 cooked blue swimmer crabs (650g)
4 cooked balmain bugs (800g)
16 cooked large prawns (1kg)
12 oysters on the half shell (300g)
3 large lemons (540g), cut into wedges

1 With lobster upside-down, cut through chest and tail with heavy knife; turn lobster around, cut through head. Pull halves apart; use small spoon to remove brain matter and liver. Rinse lobster carefully under cold water; pat dry with absorbent paper.

2 Lift tail flap off crabs, then, with a peeling motion, lift off back shell. Remove and discard the whitish gills, liver and brain matter; rinse crab well under cold water; cut crab bodies into halves.

3 Place bugs upside-down on chopping board; using heavy knife, cut in half lengthways. Remove any green matter, liver and back vein from tails.

4 Shell and devein prawns, leaving heads and tails intact.

5 Arrange seafood on large serving platter with lemon. Serve with dipping sauce of your choice.

per serving 4.6g total fat (1.1g saturated fat); 1977kJ (473 cal); 1.5g carbohydrate; 103.8g protein; 1.1g fibre

dipping sauces

SOY AND MIRIN

PREPARATION TIME 5 MINUTES
MAKES ½ cup

2 tablespoons water
1 tablespoon soy sauce
2 tablespoons mirin
2 teaspoons rice vinegar
½ teaspoon sambal oelek

Combine ingredients in small bowl.

per tablespoon
0g total fat (0g saturated fat); 27kJ (6.4 cal); 0.4g carbohydrate; 0.2g protein; 0g fibre

MUSTARD AND DILL

PREPARATION TIME 5 MINUTES
MAKES ⅔ cup

½ cup (150g) mayonnaise
1 tablespoon water
1 tablespoon drained baby capers, rinsed
1 teaspoon wholegrain mustard
1 tablespoon coarsely chopped fresh dill

Combine ingredients in small bowl.

per tablespoon
6.1g total fat (0.7g saturated fat); 297kJ (71 cal); 3.9g carbohydrate; 0.2g protein; 0.2g fibre

CHILLI AND LIME

PREPARATION TIME 5 MINUTES
MAKES ½ cup

¼ cup (60ml) sweet chilli sauce
2 tablespoons lime juice
1 tablespoon water
1 teaspoon fish sauce
2 teaspoons finely chopped fresh vietnamese mint

Combine ingredients in small bowl.

per tablespoon
0.3g total fat (0.1g saturated fat); 59kJ (14 cal); 2.2g carbohydrate; 0.2g protein; 0.5g fibre

Cold seafood platter with mustard and dill sauce.

basil and oregano steak with char-grilled vegetables

PREPARATION TIME 20 MINUTES **COOKING TIME** 30 MINUTES **SERVES** 4

2 teaspoons finely chopped
fresh oregano

¼ cup finely chopped fresh basil

1 tablespoon finely grated
lemon rind

2 tablespoons lemon juice

4 anchovy fillets, drained,
chopped finely

4 beef sirloin steaks (1kg)

2 baby fennel bulbs (260g),
quartered

3 small zucchini (270g),
chopped coarsely

1 large red capsicum (350g),
sliced thickly

200g portobello mushrooms,
sliced thickly

4 baby eggplants (240g),
chopped coarsely

2 small red onions (200g),
sliced thickly

2 teaspoons olive oil

¼ cup (60ml) lemon juice, extra

2 tablespoons fresh oregano leaves

1 Combine chopped oregano, basil, rind, the 2 tablespoons of lemon juice and anchovy in large bowl, add beef; toss beef to coat in marinade. Cover; refrigerate until required.

2 Meanwhile, combine fennel, zucchini, capsicum, mushroom, eggplant, onion and oil in large bowl; cook vegetables, in batches, on heated, lightly oiled grill plate (or grill or barbecue) until just tender. Add extra lemon juice and oregano leaves to bowl with vegetables; toss gently to combine. Cover to keep warm.

3 Cook beef mixture on same grill plate (or grill or barbecue) until cooked as desired; serve with vegetables.

per serving 26.1g total fat (10.6g saturated fat); 2153kJ (515 cal); 11g carbohydrate; 58.4g protein; 6.2g fibre

barbecued chicken with nam jim

PREPARATION TIME 15 MINUTES (PLUS STANDING TIME) COOKING TIME 20 MINUTES SERVES 4

8 chicken thigh cutlets (1.6kg)

⅓ cup (90g) grated palm sugar

2 teaspoons ground cumin

1 teaspoon salt

1 cup loosely packed fresh mint leaves

1 cup loosely packed fresh thai basil leaves

NAM JIM

2 cloves garlic, crushed

3 large green chillies, chopped

2 coriander roots

2 tablespoons fish sauce

2 tablespoons grated palm sugar

3 shallots (75g), chopped

¼ cup (60ml) lime juice

1 Cut two deep slashes through skin and flesh of chicken. Rub chicken with combined sugar, cumin and salt. Stand for 10 minutes.

2 Meanwhile, make nam jim.

3 Place chicken, skin-side down, on heated, lightly oiled grill plate (or grill or covered barbecue) on low heat about 10 minutes. Turn over, cover chicken with foil (or cover barbecue with lid); cook until chicken is cooked through.

4 Serve chicken on combined herbs with nam jim.

NAM JIM Blend or process ingredients until smooth.

tips The nam jim can be made up to two hours ahead. The chicken can be prepared several hours ahead.
Brown sugar can be substituted for palm sugar.

per serving 20.5g total fat (6.2g saturated fat); 2153kJ (515 cal);
30g carbohydrate; 53.9g protein; 2.1g fibre

osso buco

PREPARATION TIME 30 MINUTES   **COOKING TIME** 2 HOURS 30 MINUTES   **SERVES** 4

1 tablespoon olive oil

8 pieces veal osso buco (2kg)

1 medium brown onion (150g),
chopped coarsely

2 cloves garlic, crushed

1 trimmed celery stalk (100g),
chopped coarsely

1 large carrot (180g),
chopped coarsely

2 tablespoons tomato paste

½ cup (125ml) dry white wine

1 cup (250ml) beef stock

1 cup (250ml) water

400g can crushed tomatoes

1 teaspoon fresh rosemary leaves

1 medium eggplant (300g),
chopped coarsely

1 medium green capsicum (200g),
chopped coarsely

1 medium yellow capsicum (200g),
chopped coarsely

GREMOLATA

2 teaspoons finely grated
lemon rind

¼ cup finely chopped fresh
flat-leaf parsley

1 tablespoon finely chopped
fresh rosemary

1 clove garlic, chopped finely

1 Heat half of the oil in large saucepan; cook veal, in batches, until browned all over.
2 Heat remaining oil in same pan; cook onion, garlic, celery and carrot, stirring, until vegetables soften. Stir in tomato paste, wine, stock, the water, undrained tomatoes and rosemary; bring to a boil.
3 Return veal to pan, fitting pieces upright and tightly together in single layer; return to a boil. Reduce heat; simmer, covered, 1½ hours. Add eggplant; cook, uncovered, 15 minutes, stirring occasionally. Add capsicums; cook, uncovered, about 15 minutes or until vegetables are tender.
4 Meanwhile, make gremolata.
5 Remove veal and vegetables from dish; cover to keep warm. Bring sauce to a boil; boil, uncovered, about 10 minutes or until sauce thickens slightly.
6 Divide veal and vegetables among serving plates; top with sauce, sprinkle with gremolata.

GREMOLATA Combine ingredients in small bowl.

per serving 6.6g total fat (1g saturated fat); 1831kJ (438 cal); 13.6g carbohydrate; 74.7g protein; 6.6g fibre

vindaloo with raita and spicy dhal

PREPARATION TIME 40 MINUTES (PLUS REFRIGERATION TIME) **COOKING TIME** 2 HOURS **SERVES** 4

2 teaspoons cumin seeds

2 teaspoons garam masala

4 cardamom pods, bruised

4cm piece fresh ginger (20g), grated finely

6 cloves garlic, crushed

8 fresh small red thai chillies, chopped finely

2 tablespoons white vinegar

1 tablespoon tamarind concentrate

1.5kg beef chuck steak, diced into 3cm pieces

2 tablespoons ghee

2 large brown onions (400g), chopped finely

1 cinnamon stick

6 cloves

2 teaspoons plain flour

3 cups (750ml) beef stock

SPICY DHAL

2 tablespoons vegetable oil

2 cloves garlic, crushed

1cm piece fresh ginger (5g), grated finely

1 medium brown onion (150g), chopped finely

3 teaspoons chilli powder

2 teaspoons white sugar

2 teaspoons garam masala

2 teaspoons ground turmeric

1/2 teaspoon ground coriander

1 tablespoon ground cumin

1 cup (200g) red lentils

400g can crushed tomatoes

1 trimmed celery stalk (100g), sliced thinly

2 tablespoons lemon juice

2 1/2 cups (625ml) vegetable stock

1/3 cup (80ml) cream

2 tablespoons coarsely chopped fresh coriander

RAITA

1 lebanese cucumber (130g), seeded, grated coarsely, drained

1 small brown onion (80g), chopped finely

400g yogurt

1/4 teaspoon chilli powder

1 teaspoon toasted black mustard seeds

1 tablespoon coarsely chopped fresh coriander

1 tablespoon coarsely chopped fresh mint

1 Dry-fry cumin, garam masala and cardamom in large heated frying pan; stir over low heat until fragrant. Combine roasted spices with ginger, garlic, chilli, vinegar and tamarind in large bowl, add beef; toss beef to coat in marinade. Cover; refrigerate 1 hour or overnight.

2 Melt ghee in large frying pan; cook onion, cinnamon and cloves, stirring, until onion is browned lightly. Add beef mixture; cook, stirring, until beef is browned all over. Stir in flour; cook, stirring, 2 minutes. Gradually add stock; bring to a boil, stirring. Reduce heat; simmer, uncovered, 1 hour.

3 Meanwhile, make spicy dahl and raita.

4 Serve vindaloo with spicy dhal, raita and, if desired, a bowl of crisp pappadums.

SPICY DHAL Heat oil in large heavy-based saucepan; cook garlic, ginger and onion, stirring, until onion softens. Add chilli, sugar, garam masala, turmeric, coriander and cumin; cook, stirring, until fragrant. Add lentils, undrained tomatoes, celery, juice and stock; bring to a boil. Reduce heat; simmer, covered, about 30 minutes or until lentils are tender. Blend or process dhal mixture, in batches, until pureed; return to pan. Add cream and coriander; cook, stirring, until heated through.

RAITA Combine ingredients in medium bowl.

tips Both the vindaloo curry and the spicy dhal are best made a day ahead to allow their flavours to develop fully.
Round steak and skirt steak are also suitable for this recipe.

per serving 49.8g total fat (22.7g saturated fat); 4318kJ (1033 cal); 44.6g carbohydrate; 101.2g protein; 13g fibre

singapore chilli crab

PREPARATION TIME 45 MINUTES (PLUS STANDING TIME) **COOKING TIME** 45 MINUTES **SERVES** 4

2 whole uncooked mud crabs (1.5kg)

2 tablespoons peanut oil

1 fresh long red chilli, chopped finely

2 cloves garlic, crushed

2cm piece fresh ginger (10g), grated finely

⅓ cup (80ml) chinese cooking wine

400g can crushed tomatoes

1 cup (250ml) water

1 tablespoon brown sugar

2 lebanese cucumbers (260g), halved lengthways, sliced thinly

10cm piece fresh ginger (50g), sliced thinly

3 green onions, sliced thinly

¼ cup loosely packed fresh coriander leaves

2 fresh long red chillies, sliced thinly

1 Place crabs in large container filled with ice and water; stand about 1 hour. Lift tail flap off crabs, then, with a peeling motion, lift off back shell. Remove and discard the whitish gills, liver and brain matter; rinse crab well. Using heavy knife, cut crab bodies into sixths.

2 Heat oil in wok; stir-fry chopped chilli, garlic and grated ginger until fragrant. Add wine; cook until liquid has reduced by half. Add undrained tomatoes, the water and sugar; bring to a boil. Reserve half of the sauce in small bowl.

3 Add half of the crab to wok, reduce heat; simmer, covered, about 15 minutes or until crab has changed colour. Stir in half the cucumber. Transfer to large serving bowl; cover to keep warm. Repeat with reserved sauce, remaining crab and cucumber.

4 Cut sliced ginger into thin strips. Combine with onion, coriander and sliced chilli; sprinkle over crab.

tip Provide finger bowls filled with warm water and lemon slices – and plenty of large napkins – with this dish.

per serving 10.6g total fat (1.8g saturated fat); 1032kJ (247 cal); 11.1g carbohydrate; 23.8g protein; 3g fibre

crisp-skinned thai chilli snapper

PREPARATION TIME 15 MINUTES (PLUS REFRIGERATION TIME) **COOKING TIME** 45 MINUTES **SERVES** 6

1 whole snapper (1.2 kg)

4 cloves garlic, crushed

¼ cup chopped fresh lemon grass

¼ cup chopped fresh coriander

2 fresh small red thai chillies, chopped finely

2 tablespoons mild sweet chilli sauce

4cm piece fresh ginger (20g), grated finely

1 tablespoon thai red curry paste

2 tablespoons lime juice

2 tablespoons mild sweet chilli sauce, extra

½ cup firmly packed fresh coriander leaves, extra

1 Make four deep slits diagonally across both sides of fish; place fish in shallow non-metallic ovenproof dish.

2 Combine remaining ingredients, except extra chilli sauce and extra coriander leaves, in medium bowl. Pour over fish; cover, refrigerate 3 hours or overnight.

3 Preheat oven to moderate (180°C/160°C fan-forced).

4 Cover dish with foil; bake in moderate oven about 35 minutes or until fish is almost tender.

5 Brush fish with extra chilli sauce then grill about 10 minutes or until skin is browned and crisp. Serve topped with coriander leaves.

per serving 2.9g total fat (0.7g saturated fat); 447kJ (107 cal); 3.6g carbohydrate; 16.1g protein; 1.8g fibre

pork ribs with chorizo and smoked paprika

PREPARATION TIME 15 MINUTES **COOKING TIME** 2 HOURS **SERVES** 4

1.5kg American-style pork ribs

4 cloves garlic, crushed

2 teaspoons smoked paprika

1 tablespoon olive oil

200g chorizo, sliced thinly

1 tablespoon olive oil, extra

1 medium red onion (170g),
chopped coarsely

1 medium red capsicum (200g),
chopped coarsely

1 tablespoon brown sugar

800g can chopped tomatoes

1 cup (250ml) chicken stock

1 Cut between bones of pork to separate into individual ribs. Combine garlic,
    paprika and olive oil in small bowl; rub over pork ribs.
2 Preheat oven to moderately slow (160°C/140°C fan-forced).
3 Cook chorizo in heated large flameproof baking dish, stirring, until browned
    lightly. Remove from dish with slotted spoon; drain on absorbent paper.
4 Cook ribs, in same dish, in batches, until well browned all over. Drain ribs on
    absorbent paper.
5 Add extra olive oil, onion and capsicum to same dish; cook, stirring, until
    onion is soft. Return ribs and chorizo to dish; add sugar, undrained tomatoes
    and stock, bring to a boil.
6 Cover dish tightly with foil, bake in moderately slow oven 1 hour. Remove foil,
    bake further 30 minutes or until ribs are tender.

tip This recipe can be made a day ahead.

per serving 38.5g total fat (11.4g saturated fat); 2516kJ (602 cal);
15.6g carbohydrate; 49.2g protein; 4.1g fibre

roast lamb with anchovies, garlic and vegetables

PREPARATION TIME 25 MINUTES **COOKING TIME** 1 HOUR 25 MINUTES **SERVES** 4

45g can anchovy fillets

1.5kg Easy Carve leg of lamb

1 tablespoon fresh rosemary leaves

2 cloves garlic, sliced thinly

2 bulbs garlic, halved horizontally, extra

4 small parsnips (480g)

2 tablespoons olive oil

500g asparagus

12 small truss tomatoes

¼ cup (60ml) red wine

1 tablespoon balsamic vinegar

1 cup (250ml) beef stock

1 Preheat oven to moderate (180°C/160°C fan-forced). Drain anchovies over a small bowl; reserve oil. Chop anchovies coarsely.

2 Using the point of a sharp knife, pierce the lamb about 12 times all over, gently twisting to make a small hole. Press anchovies, rosemary and sliced garlic evenly into the holes. Place lamb on a rack in baking dish. Pour anchovy oil over lamb.

3 Roast lamb in moderate oven about 1 hour 10 minutes or until lamb is cooked as desired.

4 Meanwhile, place extra garlic and parsnips in separate baking dish, drizzle with half of the olive oil; bake with lamb 40 minutes. Add asparagus, tomatoes and remaining oil, bake further 10 minutes or until vegetables are tender.

5 Remove lamb from dish; cover lamb, stand 10 minutes. Drain fat from dish; place baking dish over medium heat. Add wine; bring to a boil. Add balsamic vinegar, stock and any juices collected from lamb; cook, stirring, until sauce boils and reduces to 1 cup. Serve lamb with vegetables and sauce.

tip The lamb can be prepared several hours ahead. Recipe is best cooked close to serving.

per serving 31.9g total fat (10.8g saturated fat); 3077kJ (736 cal); 16.6g carbohydrate; 93g protein; 10.8g fibre

pizza trio

PREPARATION TIME 40 MINUTES (PLUS STANDING TIME) **COOKING TIME** 10 MINUTES **MAKES** 3 THIN PIZZAS
Each topping quantity given is enough for one pizza. Each pizza makes approximately five slices.

PIZZA DOUGH

2 teaspoons (7g) dry yeast
½ teaspoon caster sugar
¾ cup (180ml) warm water
2 cups (300g) plain flour
1 teaspoon salt
2 tablespoons olive oil
3 teaspoons olive oil, extra

ANCHOVY OLIVE TOPPING

2 teaspoons olive oil
⅓ cup (80ml) tomato pasta sauce
7 anchovy fillets, halved
¼ cup (30g) black olives,
pitted, halved
12 fresh basil leaves

PANCETTA TOPPING

2 teaspoons olive oil
⅓ cup (80ml) tomato pasta sauce
2 cloves garlic, sliced thinly
½ cup (40g) parmesan cheese flakes
6 thin slices chilli pancetta (90g)

SPICY SAUSAGE TOPPING

2 teaspoons olive oil
⅓ cup (80ml) tomato pasta sauce
175g cooked spicy italian sausage
1 fresh long red thai chilli,
sliced thinly
¼ cup (30g) black olives,
pitted, halved
100g bocconcini or mozzarella
cheese, sliced
2 tablespoons fresh oregano leaves

1 To make pizza dough, combine yeast, sugar and water in small bowl; cover, stand in warm place about 10 minutes or until frothy. Sift flour and salt into large bowl; stir in yeast mixture and oil; mix to a soft dough. Bring dough together with your hands and add a little extra water, if needed, until ingredients are combined.

2 Knead dough on lightly floured surface about 10 minutes or until smooth and elastic, pushing the dough with the heel of your hand and giving it a quarter turn each time. Place dough in lightly oiled large bowl; cover, stand in warm place about 1 hour or until doubled in size.

3 Meanwhile, preheat a covered barbecue.

4 Punch dough down with your fist, then knead on lightly floured surface until smooth. Divide dough into three portions.

5 Roll each portion to about a 16cm x 40 cm rectangle.

6 Layer two pieces of aluminium foil large enough to fit one rectangle of dough. Brush foil with 1 teaspoon of the extra oil. Place one portion of dough on top; repeat with extra foil and remaining oil and dough.

7 Turn off burners underneath middle grill plate, leaving outer burners on to cook by indirect heat. Place pizzas on foil on grill plate; cover barbecue, cook about 4 minutes or until underneath is browned. (If dough puffs up, flatten quickly with an egg slide.)

8 Carefully remove pizza bases from barbecue, close cover. Turn pizza bases over on foil, brush cooked side with oil, then spread with pasta sauce; top with selected ingredients for each topping except the fresh herbs. Return pizzas to barbecue on foil; cover barbecue, cook 5 minutes or until well browned underneath and crisp. Serve pizzas sprinkled with herbs.

tips Pizzas are best made close to serving.
Pizza dough also can be made in breadmaker, following manufacturer's directions.
Cooking the pizza in a covered barbecue gives it a wonderful smoky flavour similar to a wood-fired oven. If you don't have a covered barbecue, pizza can be cooked in the oven. Place toppings on dough and bake until browned and crisp. There is no need to turn the dough over using this method.

ANCHOVY OLIVE TOPPING
per slice 6.1g total fat (0.9g saturated fat); 598kJ (143 cal); 17.8g carbohydrate; 4.1g protein; 1.3g fibre

PANCETTA TOPPING
per slice 10.7g total fat (3.4g saturated fat); 832kJ (199 cal); 16.7g carbohydrate; 9.2g protein; 1.4g fibre

SPICY SAUSAGE TOPPING
per slice 18.4g total fat (6.4g saturated fat); 1158kJ (277 cal); 18g carbohydrate; 10.3g protein; 1.4g fibre

chiang mai noodles

PREPARATION TIME 20 MINUTES **COOKING TIME** 25 MINUTES **SERVES** 4

vegetable oil, for deep-frying

500g fresh egg noodles

1 large brown onion (200g), sliced thinly

2 green onions, sliced thinly

¼ cup loosely packed fresh coriander leaves

¼ cup (75g) red curry paste

2 cloves garlic, crushed

¼ teaspoon ground turmeric

2 cups (500ml) water

400ml can coconut milk

500g chicken breast fillets, sliced thinly

¼ cup (60ml) fish sauce

1 tablespoon soy sauce

2 tablespoons grated palm sugar

2 teaspoons lime juice

2 tablespoons coarsely chopped fresh coriander

1 fresh long red thai chilli, sliced thinly

1 Heat oil in wok; deep-fry 100g of the noodles, in batches, until crisp. Drain on absorbent paper.

2 Using same heated oil, deep-fry brown onion, in batches, until browned lightly and crisp. Drain on absorbent paper. Combine fried noodles, fried onion, green onion and coriander leaves in small bowl. Cool oil; remove from wok, reserve for another use.

3 Place remaining noodles in large heatproof bowl, cover with boiling water; use fork to separate noodles, drain.

4 Cook paste, garlic and turmeric in same cleaned wok, add the water and coconut milk; bring to a boil. Reduce heat; simmer, stirring, 2 minutes. Add chicken; cook, stirring, about 5 minutes or until chicken is cooked through. Add sauces, sugar and juice; cook, stirring, until sugar dissolves. Stir in chopped coriander.

5 Divide drained noodles among serving bowls; spoon chicken curry mixture into each bowl, top with fried noodle mixture. Sprinkle chilli slices over each bowl.

tip Substitute brown sugar for the palm sugar, if desired.

per serving 34.7g total fat (20.2g saturated fat); 3394kJ (812 cal); 79.4g carbohydrate; 45.3g protein; 7.6g fibre

char-grilled beef salad

PREPARATION TIME 15 MINUTES (PLUS REFRIGERATION TIME) **COOKING TIME** 10 MINUTES **SERVES** 4

500g beef rump steak

¼ cup (60ml) fish sauce

¼ cup (60ml) lime juice

3 lebanese cucumbers (390g), seeded, sliced thinly

4 fresh small red thai chillies, sliced thinly

8 green onions, sliced thinly

250g cherry tomatoes, quartered

I cup loosely packed fresh vietnamese mint leaves

I cup loosely packed fresh coriander leaves

I tablespoon grated palm sugar

I tablespoon soy sauce

I clove garlic, crushed

1 Combine beef with 2 tablespoons of the fish sauce and 1 tablespoon of the juice in large bowl; cover, refrigerate 3 hours or overnight.

2 Drain beef; discard marinade. Cook beef on heated, oiled grill plate (or grill or barbecue) until browned and cooked as desired. Cover beef, stand 5 minutes; slice thinly.

3 Meanwhile, combine cucumber, chilli, onion, tomato and herbs in large bowl. Combine remaining fish sauce and remaining juice with sugar, soy sauce and garlic in screw-top jar; shake well.

4 Add beef and dressing to salad; toss gently.

tips Substitute brown sugar for the palm sugar, if desired.
The salad dressing can be made a day ahead and kept, covered, in the refrigerator.

per serving 8.7g total fat (3.8g saturated fat); 991kJ (237 cal); 8.1g carbohydrate; 30.9g protein; 3.8g fibre

asian chicken broth

PREPARATION TIME 30 MINUTES **COOKING TIME** 20 MINUTES **SERVES** 4

1 litre (4 cups) water

1 litre (4 cups) chicken stock

10cm stick (20g) fresh lemon grass, chopped finely

4cm piece fresh ginger (20g), sliced thinly

2 fresh small red thai chillies, sliced thinly

2 tablespoons soy sauce

1 tablespoon lime juice

1 tablespoon fish sauce

500g choy sum, chopped coarsely

3 green onions, sliced thinly

⅓ cup loosely packed fresh coriander leaves

CHICKEN DUMPLINGS

400g chicken mince

1 tablespoon finely chopped fresh coriander

2 cloves garlic, crushed

1 Combine the water, stock, lemon grass, ginger, chilli and soy sauce in large saucepan; bring to a boil. Reduce heat; simmer, uncovered, about 5 minutes.

2 Meanwhile, make chicken dumplings.

3 Add chicken dumplings to simmering broth; simmer, covered, about 5 minutes or until dumplings are cooked through.

4 Add juice, fish sauce, choy sum and onion to broth; cook, uncovered, until choy sum just wilts. Stir in coriander just before serving.

CHICKEN DUMPLINGS Combine ingredients in medium bowl. Using hands, roll level tablespoons of the mixture into balls.

per serving 9.5g total fat (2.9g saturated fat); 849kJ (203 cal); 4.4g carbohydrate; 24.8g protein; 2.5g fibre

orecchietti with lamb and peas

PREPARATION TIME 25 MINUTES **COOKING TIME** 35 MINUTES **SERVES** 4

2 tablespoons olive oil

1 medium brown onion (150g), chopped finely

1 clove garlic, crushed

600g lamb mince

2 fresh small red thai chillies, sliced thinly

500g orecchietti pasta

2 cups (300g) shelled fresh peas

3 medium tomatoes (450g), seeded, chopped finely

⅓ cup (80ml) extra virgin olive oil

GREMOLATA

½ cup finely chopped fresh flat-leaf parsley

1 clove garlic, crushed

2 teaspoons finely grated lemon rind

1 Make gremolata.
2 Heat oil in large frying pan; add onion and garlic, cook, stirring, until onion
   is soft. Add lamb and chilli; cook, stirring, about 10 minutes or until lamb is
   well browned. Cover to keep warm.
3 Meanwhile, cook pasta in large saucepan of boiling water, uncovered, until
   just tender. Reserve ¼ cup (60ml) of the cooking liquid; drain pasta.
4 Boil, steam or microwave peas until tender; drain.
5 Toss pasta in large bowl with lamb mixture, peas, reserved liquid, tomato
   and oil. Serve sprinkled with gremolata.

GREMOLATA Combine all ingredients in small bowl.

tips You will need about 800g fresh peas in the pod for this recipe.
The mince mixture and gremolata can be prepared several hours ahead.
Reheat mince just before serving.

per serving 39.5g total fat (8.8g saturated fat); 3929kJ (940 cal);
95.3g carbohydrate; 50.3g protein; 10.1g fibre

twice-fried sichuan beef

PREPARATION TIME 20 MINUTES **COOKING TIME** 30 MINUTES **SERVES** 4

600g piece beef eye fillet, sliced thinly

2 tablespoons dry sherry

2 tablespoons salt-reduced soy sauce

1 teaspoon brown sugar

½ cup (75g) cornflour

1½ cups (300g) jasmine rice

vegetable oil, for deep-frying

2 teaspoons sesame oil

1 clove garlic, crushed

1 fresh small red thai chilli, chopped finely

1 medium brown onion (150g), sliced thickly

1 medium carrot (120g), halved, sliced thinly

1 small red capsicum (150g), sliced thinly

500g gai larn, chopped coarsely

1 tablespoon cracked sichuan peppercorns

2 tablespoons oyster sauce

¼ cup (60ml) salt-reduced soy sauce, extra

½ cup (125ml) beef stock

2 teaspoons brown sugar, extra

1 Combine beef, sherry, soy sauce and sugar in medium bowl. Stand 10 minutes; drain. Toss beef in cornflour; shake off excess.

2 Meanwhile, cook rice in large saucepan of boiling water, uncovered, until just tender; drain. Cover to keep warm.

3 Heat vegetable oil in wok; deep-fry beef, in batches, until crisp. Drain on absorbent paper. Reserve oil for another use.

4 Heat sesame oil in same cleaned wok; stir-fry garlic, chilli and onion until onion softens. Add carrot and capsicum; stir-fry until just tender. Add gai larn; stir-fry until just wilted. Add beef, peppercorns, oyster sauce, extra soy sauce, stock and extra sugar; stir-fry until heated through. Serve beef and vegetables with rice.

tip It is easier to slice beef thinly if it is partially frozen.

per serving 17.2g total fat (3.9g saturated fat); 2976kJ (712 cal); 93.4g carbohydrate; 42.3g protein; 5.6g fibre

prawn and fennel risotto

PREPARATION TIME 30 MINUTES **COOKING TIME** 45 MINUTES **SERVES** 4

600g uncooked small prawns

1 litre (4 cups) chicken or fish stock

2 cups (500ml) water

pinch of saffron threads

¼ cup (60ml) olive oil

1 small fennel bulb (200g),
sliced thinly

1 medium brown onion (150g),
chopped finely

2 cloves garlic, crushed

2 cups (400g) arborio rice

½ cup (125ml) dry white wine

¼ teaspoon dried chilli flakes,
optional

30g butter

2 tablespoons chopped fennel tips

1 Shell and devein prawns leaving tails intact. Place stock, the water and saffron in large saucepan. Bring to a boil, reduce to a simmer; cover.

2 Meanwhile, heat oil in large saucepan; add fennel, cook, stirring, until fennel is tender. Remove fennel from pan with slotted spoon. Add prawns to same pan; cook, stirring, until prawns just change colour. Remove from pan with slotted spoon. Add onion and garlic to same pan; cook, stirring, until onion is soft.

3 Add rice to pan, stir about 1 minute or until rice is well coated. Add wine to pan, bring to a boil; simmer, uncovered, until most of the wine has evaporated.

4 Stir in ½ cup (125ml) hot stock; cook, stirring, over medium heat until liquid is absorbed. Continue adding stock in ½-cup batches, stirring until absorbed after each addition. Cooking time should be about 25 minutes, or until rice is just tender.

5 Return fennel to pan with prawns and chilli; cook, stirring, until hot. Stir in butter and fennel tips.

tips This recipe is best made just before serving.
When preparing the fennel, reserve the tips to use in the recipe.

per serving 21.9g total fat (6.7g saturated fat); 2738kJ (655 cal);
83.5g carbohydrate; 25.8g protein; 3.8g fibre

spaghetti with clams

PREPARATION TIME 15 MINUTES (PLUS STANDING TIME) **COOKING TIME** 20 MINUTES **SERVES** 4

1kg clams

¼ cup (60ml) dry white wine

500g spaghetti

½ cup (125ml) extra virgin olive oil

2 cloves garlic, crushed

2 fresh medium red chillies, chopped finely

½ cup coarsely chopped fresh flat-leaf parsley

1 Rinse clams. Place in large bowl of cold water for 1 hour; drain.

2 Place wine in large saucepan; bring to a boil. Add clams; simmer, covered, until shells open (discard any that don't). Remove clams from pan; cover to keep warm. Strain cooking liquid through fine sieve into jug; reserve ½ cup (125ml) of the liquid.

3 Cook spaghetti in large saucepan of boiling water until tender; drain. Return spaghetti to pan.

4 Meanwhile, heat oil in frying pan; add garlic and chilli, cook, stirring, until fragrant.

5 Add clams to spaghetti with garlic mixture, parsley and enough of the reserved cooking liquid to moisten mixture; toss gently.

tip This recipe is best made just before serving.

per serving 30.1g total fat (4.3g saturated fat); 3005kJ (719 cal); 86.2g carbohydrate; 23g protein; 4.7g fibre

vegetable curry with yogurt

PREPARATION TIME 25 MINUTES **COOKING TIME** 15 MINUTES **SERVES** 4

2 teaspoons vegetable oil

4cm piece fresh ginger (20g), grated

3 green onions, sliced thinly

2 cloves garlic, crushed

1 long green chilli, chopped finely

¼ teaspoon ground cardamom

1 teaspoon garam masala

1 tablespoon curry powder

1 teaspoon ground turmeric

2 medium green apples (300g),
grated coarsely

1 tablespoon lemon juice

2 cups (500ml) vegetable stock

½ small cauliflower (500g),
cut into florets

4 yellow patty-pan squash (120g),
halved

2 small zucchini (180g),
sliced thickly

150g baby spinach leaves

200g low-fat yogurt

1 Heat oil in large saucepan; cook ginger, onion, garlic, chilli, cardamom, garam masala, curry powder and turmeric until fragrant. Add apple, juice and stock; cook, uncovered, 5 minutes, stirring occasionally.

2 Add cauliflower, squash and zucchini; cook, uncovered, until vegetables are just tender. Remove from heat; stir in spinach and yogurt just before serving.

per serving 3.8g total fat (0.6g saturated fat); 285kJ (140 cal); 16g carbohydrate; 9.8g protein; 6.6g fibre

seafood laksa

PREPARATION TIME 35 MINUTES **COOKING TIME** 30 MINUTES **SERVES** 6

250g uncooked medium prawns
1 blue swimmer crab (325g)
10 small black mussels (250g)
2 small squid hoods (300g)
300g firm white fish fillets
1 tablespoon peanut oil
1 litre (4 cups) fish stock
400g can coconut milk
500g fresh rice noodles
2 tablespoons lime juice
1 tablespoon fish sauce
80g fresh mint leaves
1 cup (80g) bean sprouts

LAKSA PASTE
2 cloves garlic, sliced
4 spring onions, chopped coarsely
4 fresh small red thai chillies,
chopped coarsely
4 coriander roots, chopped coarsely
10cm stick (20g) fresh lemon grass,
chopped coarsely
4cm piece fresh ginger (20g),
chopped coarsely
1 tablespoon sesame oil
1 teaspoon shrimp paste
½ teaspoon ground turmeric
1 tablespoon ground cumin
1 teaspoon sea salt
1 teaspoon brown sugar

1   Make laksa paste.
2   Shell and devein prawns leaving tails intact. Lift tail flap off crab, then, with a peeling motion, lift off back shell. Remove and discard the whitish gills, liver and brain matter; rinse crab well under cold water. Cut crab in half through the centre of the body. Remove claws, cut body in half again. Scrub mussels and remove beards. Cut cleaned squid down one side to open out flat. Score inside surface in a criss-cross pattern; cut into strips. Cut fish into 3cm pieces.
3   Heat oil in wok; cook laksa paste, stirring constantly, until fragrant. Add stock, bring to a boil; reduce heat, simmer, uncovered, 5 minutes.
4   Add coconut milk, bring to a boil; add crab, simmer, uncovered, until beginning to change colour. Add mussels, stir through. Return to simmer, add prawns, squid and fish; simmer, uncovered, until seafood is just cooked through.
5   Meanwhile, rinse noodles in hot water until separated.
6   Remove laksa from heat, add juice and sauce.
7   Divide noodles among serving bowls and ladle soup over top. Top with mint leaves and bean sprouts; serve with chilli or sambal oelek, if desired.

LAKSA PASTE   Blend or process ingredients to form a paste.

tip The laksa paste can be made several days ahead and kept, covered, in the refrigerator.

per serving 21.8g total fat (13.3g saturated fat); 1956kJ (468 cal); 40.4g carbohydrate; 27.3g protein; 3.8g fibre

chocolate self-saucing pudding

PREPARATION TIME 10 MINUTES **COOKING TIME** 40 MINUTES **SERVES** 6

1 cup (150g) self-raising flour
½ teaspoon bicarbonate of soda
½ cup (50g) cocoa powder
1¼ cups (275g) firmly packed brown sugar
80g butter, melted
½ cup (120g) sour cream
1 egg, beaten lightly
2 cups (500ml) boiling water

1 Preheat oven to moderate (180°C/160°C fan-forced). Grease deep 1.5-litre (6-cup) ovenproof dish.
2 Sift flour, soda, half of the cocoa and ½ cup of the sugar into medium bowl; stir in combined butter, sour cream and egg.
3 Spread mixture into prepared dish. Sift remaining cocoa and remaining sugar evenly over mixture; gently pour over the boiling water. Bake, uncovered, in moderate oven about 40 minutes. Stand 5 minutes before serving.

tip Serve with vanilla ice-cream, if desired.

per serving 21.2g total fat (13.4g saturated fat); 1935kJ (763 cal); 64.7g carbohydrate; 5.8g protein; 1.3g fibre

berry custard pastries

PREPARATION TIME 40 MINUTES (PLUS REFRIGERATION TIME) **COOKING TIME** 12 MINUTES **SERVES** 8

2 sheets ready-rolled
butter puff pastry
2 tablespoons icing sugar mixture
700g mixed fresh berries

CUSTARD CREAM
300ml thickened cream
300g thick vanilla custard
¼ cup (40g) icing sugar mixture

1 Preheat oven to hot (220°C/200°C fan-forced). Grease and line three oven trays with baking paper.

2 Cut one pastry sheet in half. Sprinkle one half with 2 teaspoons of the sifted icing sugar; place remaining pastry half on top. Roll pastry up tightly from short side; cut log into eight rounds. Repeat with remaining pastry sheet and another 2 teaspoons of the icing sugar.

3 Place rounds, cut-side up, on board dusted lightly with icing sugar; roll out each round into an oval shape about 8cm x 10cm.

4 Place ovals on prepared trays. Bake, uncovered, in hot oven about 12 minutes or until pastries are browned lightly and crisp, turning halfway through baking.

5 Meanwhile, make the custard cream.

6 Place a drop of the custard cream on each of eight plates (to stop pastry sliding); top each with one pastry. Divide half of the berries over pastries, then top with custard cream, remaining berries and remaining pastries. Dust with remaining sifted icing sugar.

CUSTARD CREAM Beat ingredients in small bowl with electric mixer until soft peaks form. Cover; refrigerate 30 minutes or until firm.

tips This recipe can be prepared a day ahead. Assemble just before serving. Keep pastries in an airtight container and the custard cream, covered, in the refrigerator.

per serving 24.5g total fat (14.9g saturated fat); 1534kJ (367 cal); 31.9g carbohydrate; 5.9g protein; 2.6g fibre

bread and butter pudding cake

PREPARATION TIME 40 MINUTES (PLUS STANDING TIME)
COOKING TIME 1 HOUR 20 MINUTES (PLUS COOLING TIME) **SERVES** 12

⅓ cup (55g) sultanas
⅓ cup (55g) raisins
⅓ cup (50g) coarsely chopped
dried apricots
¼ cup (35g) dried currants
⅓ cup (65g) chopped dried figs
2 tablespoons mixed peel
¼ cup (60ml) brandy
2 tablespoons orange juice
2 small brioche (200g)
80g butter, melted
¼ cup (80g) apricot jam, warmed
1 tablespoon icing sugar mixture

SPONGE
4 eggs
½ cup (110g) caster sugar
¾ cup (110g) self-raising flour
50g butter, melted

CUSTARD
300ml thickened cream
1 cup (250ml) milk
2 eggs
4 egg yolks
½ cup (110g) caster sugar

1 Combine dried fruits, peel, brandy and juice in medium bowl, cover; stand overnight.
2 Preheat oven to moderately hot (200°C/180°C fan-forced). Grease and flour deep 22cm-round cake pan.
3 Make sponge. Make custard.
4 Decrease oven to moderately slow (160°C/140°C fan-forced).
5 Grease same cleaned cake pan; line base and side with baking paper, extending paper 5cm above edge of pan. Cut each brioche vertically into six slices; brush slices on both sides with a quarter of the combined butter and jam.
6 Using serrated knife, split cake into three layers; place bottom layer in prepared pan, brush with another quarter of the jam mixture. Using 6cm cutter, cut eight rounds from middle layer; brush rounds on both sides with another quarter of the jam mixture, reserve. Chop remaining cake layer coarsely.
7 Layer half of the brioche then fruit mixture, chopped cake and remaining brioche slices in pan. Pour over remaining jam mixture. Pour hot custard over layered ingredients; top with reserved rounds. Bake, uncovered, in moderately slow oven 30 minutes. Cover with foil; bake further 30 minutes; turn, top-side up, onto serving plate. Dust with sifted icing sugar.

SPONGE Beat eggs and sugar in small bowl with electric mixer until thick and creamy; transfer to large bowl. Gently fold in triple-sifted flour and butter. Pour mixture into prepared pan; bake, uncovered, in moderately hot oven about 20 minutes. Turn cake onto wire rack immediately to cool. (Can be made ahead to this stage. Cover; refrigerate overnight.)

CUSTARD Stir cream and milk in small saucepan over heat until almost boiling. Whisk eggs, yolks and sugar in large bowl. Whisking constantly, gradually add hot cream mixture to egg mixture; whisk until combined.

tip You can use a purchased sponge cake, if you prefer.

per serving 25.6g total fat (14.7g saturated fat); 2023kJ (484 cal); 54.5g carbohydrate; 8.7g protein; 2.5g fibre

white chocolate fondue

PREPARATION TIME 10 MINUTES **COOKING TIME** 5 MINUTES **SERVES** 4

180g white eating chocolate, chopped coarsely

½ cup (125ml) cream

1 tablespoon coconut-flavoured liqueur

1 cup (130g) strawberries

1 large banana (230g), chopped coarsely

150g fresh pineapple, chopped coarsely

8 slices (35g) almond bread

16 (100g) marshmallows

1 Combine chocolate and cream in small saucepan, stir over low heat until smooth; stir in liqueur. Transfer fondue to serving bowl.
2 Place fondue in centre of dining table; serve with remaining ingredients on a platter.

tip Fondue can be served with any of your favourite fruits. Provide your guests with skewers so they are able to spear the fruit and marshmallows and dip them into the chocolate pot.

per serving 13.4g total fat (8.4g saturated fat); 999kJ (239 cal); 28g carbohydrate; 3.4g protein; 1.1g fibre

little kaffir lime syrup cakes

PREPARATION TIME 10 MINUTES **COOKING TIME** 25 MINUTES **MAKES** 6

125g butter, chopped
½ cup (110g) caster sugar
2 teaspoons grated lime rind
(not kaffir lime)
2 eggs
1 cup (150g) self-raising flour
½ cup (125ml) buttermilk

LIME SYRUP
4 kaffir lime leaves, shredded
⅓ cup (80ml) lime juice
(not kaffir lime)
½ cup (110g) caster sugar
2 tablespoons water
1 teaspoon grated lime rind
(not kaffir lime)

1 Preheat oven to moderate (180°C/160°C fan-forced). Grease a six-hole mini fluted tube pan or texas (¾-cup/180ml) muffin pan.

2 Beat butter, sugar and rind in small bowl with electric mixer until light and fluffy. Add eggs, one at a time, beating until just combined between additions.

3 Transfer mixture to medium bowl; stir in sifted flour and buttermilk.

4 Divide mixture among prepared holes, smooth tops. Bake in moderate oven about 25 minutes.

5 Meanwhile, make lime syrup.

6 Stand cakes 5 minutes before turning onto wire rack over a tray. Pour hot lime syrup evenly over hot cakes. Serve cakes warm or cooled with whipped cream, if desired.

LIME SYRUP Combine all ingredients except grated lime rind in small saucepan; stir over low heat until sugar dissolved. Bring to a boil; remove from heat. Strain into medium heatproof jug. Stir in grated lime rind.

tips Recipe is best made on day of serving.
While the leaves of the kaffir lime have a unique aromatic flavour, the fruit itself does not supply much juice, so use a normal lime for the juice and rind in this recipe.
If buttermilk is unavailable, substitute ½ cup (125ml) reduced-fat milk combined with 2 teaspoons lemon juice.

per cake 19.6g total fat (12.1g saturated fat); 1743kJ (417 cal); 55.8g carbohydrate; 5.8g protein; 1g fibre

hazelnut praline tiramisu

PREPARATION TIME 40 MINUTES (PLUS STANDING TIME)
COOKING TIME 10 MINUTES (PLUS REFRIGERATION TIME) **SERVES** 15

¼ cup (30g) ground coffee
2 cups (500ml) boiling water
1 cup (250ml) marsala
4 egg yolks
¼ cup (55g) caster sugar
1kg (4 cups) mascarpone
¼ cup (60ml) marsala, extra
½ cup (110g) caster sugar, extra
500g sponge finger biscuits
100g coarsely grated dark
eating chocolate

HAZELNUT PRALINE
¼ cup (35g) hazelnuts
⅓ cup (75g) caster sugar
2 tablespoons water

1 Using coffee and the boiling water, prepare coffee in a plunger. Stand for 2 minutes, plunge coffee (or combine coffee and the water in a heatproof jug, stand for 2 minutes then strain through a fine sieve); pour into large jug, stir in liqueur.

2 Beat egg yolks and sugar in small bowl with electric mixer until fluffy.

3 Beat mascarpone, extra liqueur and extra sugar in large bowl until slightly thickened. Gently fold in egg yolk mixture.

4 Pour half the coffee mixture into shallow bowl. Dip half the biscuits, a couple at a time, into coffee mixture until beginning to soften. Line base of 3-litre (12-cup) serving dish with biscuits; brush with any unused coffee mixture. Spread biscuits with half the mascarpone mixture and sprinkle with half the grated chocolate. Repeat with remaining biscuits, coffee mixture and mascarpone. Cover mixture, refrigerate overnight.

5 Make hazelnut praline.

6 Just before serving, sprinkle with remaining chocolate and chopped hazelnut praline.

HAZELNUT PRALINE Preheat oven to moderate (180°C/160°C fan-forced). Place hazelnuts in shallow baking dish; bake about 8 minutes or until skins split. Rub nuts in tea towel to remove most of the skin; cool. Lightly grease oven tray. Combine sugar and the water in small saucepan; stir over low heat until sugar is dissolved. Brush side of pan with pastry brush dipped in water to remove sugar crystals. Bring to a boil. Boil, uncovered, without stirring, about 5 minutes or until mixture turns a toffee colour. Remove from heat, stir in nuts then quickly pour onto prepared tray. Stand until set.

tips Tiramisu is best prepared a day ahead. Hazelnut praline can be made several days ahead; store in an airtight container.
Use a blender or food processor to roughly chop the praline.

per serving 47.4g total fat (29.7g saturated fat); 2838kJ (679 cal); 53.7g carbohydrate; 9.3g protein; 1g fibre

decadent chocolate roulade

PREPARATION TIME 15 MINUTES (PLUS REFRIGERATION TIME) **COOKING TIME** 20 MINUTES (PLUS COOLING TIME) **SERVES** 8

1 tablespoon caster sugar
200g dark eating chocolate, chopped
¼ cup (60ml) hot water
1 teaspoon dry instant coffee
4 eggs, separated
½ cup (110g) caster sugar, extra
300ml thickened cream
120g raspberries

1 Preheat oven to moderate (180°C/160°C fan-forced). Grease 25cm x 30cm swiss roll pan; line base with baking paper, extending paper 5cm over two long sides of pan. Place a piece of baking paper, cut the same size as swiss roll pan, on bench; sprinkle evenly with caster sugar.

2 Combine chocolate, the hot water and coffee in medium heatproof bowl. Stir over medium saucepan of simmering water until smooth; remove from heat.

3 Beat egg yolks and extra sugar in small bowl with an electric mixer until thick and creamy. Fold egg mixture into warm chocolate mixture.

4 Beat egg whites in small clean bowl with electric mixer until soft peaks form. Gently fold egg whites, in two batches, into chocolate mixture. Spread into prepared pan; bake in moderate oven about 15 minutes.

5 Turn cake onto sugared paper, peeling baking paper away; use serrated knife to cut away crisp edges from all sides. Cover cake with tea towel; cool.

6 Beat cream in small bowl with electric mixer until firm peaks form. Spread cake evenly with cream; sprinkle evenly with raspberries. Roll cake, from long side, by lifting paper and using it to guide the roll into log shape. Cover roll; refrigerate 30 minutes before serving.

per serving 31.5g total fat (18.8g saturated fat); 2023kJ (484 cal); 45.4g carbohydrate; 7.5g protein; 1.8g fibre

entertaining

marinated bocconcini with prosciutto

PREPARATION TIME 20 MINUTES (PLUS STANDING TIME) **MAKES** 40

2 cloves garlic, crushed
1 long green chilli, chopped
⅓ cup (80ml) olive oil
40 cherry bocconcini (600g)
10 slices (150g) thin prosciutto
1 bunch fresh basil leaves

1 Combine garlic, chilli and oil in medium bowl; add bocconcini, mix well. Stand 30 minutes.

2 Cut prosciutto slices in half crossways, then halve again lengthways.

3 Drain bocconcini from marinade; reserve marinade. Wrap a piece of prosciutto and a basil leaf around each bocconcini; secure with a toothpick.

4 Serve drizzled with reserved marinade.

tip Bocconcini can be marinated overnight.

per ball 3.8g total fat (1.4g saturated fat); 188kJ (45 cal); 0.1g carbohydrate; 2.8g protein; 0.3g fibre

cheese balls with four coatings

PREPARATION TIME 40 MINUTES (PLUS REFRIGERATION TIME) **MAKES** 64

500g neufchâtel cheese
500g farm cheese
2 teaspoons finely grated lemon rind
2 tablespoons lemon juice
¼ teaspoon sea salt

1 Line four oven trays with baking paper.
2 Blend or process ingredients until smooth; refrigerate about 2 hours or until firm enough to roll.
3 Using hands, roll rounded teaspoons of the mixture into balls; place 16 balls on each prepared tray. Refrigerate, covered, until firm.
4 Roll 16 balls in each of the four coatings. Serve cold.

tip Farm cheese can be found in the cheese section of the supermarket delicatessen or in specialty cheese shops.

PEPPER COATING

Coat balls in a mixture of 1½ tablespoons poppy seeds and 2 teaspoons cracked black pepper.

tip Pepper coating can be prepared a day ahead. Store at room temperature in an airtight container.

per ball 4.9g total fat (2.9g saturated fat); 234kJ (56 cal); 0.3g carbohydrate; 2.8g protein; 0.3g fibre

PARSLEY COATING

Coat balls in ¼ cup finely chopped fresh flat-leaf parsley.

per ball 4.4g total fat (2.8g saturated fat); 209kJ (50 cal); 0.2g carbohydrate; 2.6g protein; 0g fibre

SESAME SEED COATING

Coat balls in ¼ cup (35g) sesame seeds.

per ball 5.6g total fat (3g saturated fat); 263kJ (63 cal); 0.2g carbohydrate; 3.1g protein; 0.2g fibre

ZA'ATAR COATING

Combine 1 tablespoon each of sumac and toasted sesame seeds, 1 teaspoon each of dried oregano, dried marjoram and sweet paprika, and 2 teaspoons dried thyme; coat balls in mix.

tips Za'atar coating can be prepared a day ahead. Store at room temperature in an airtight container.
Za'atar, a Middle-Eastern spice blend, can be purchased from Middle-Eastern specialty stores.

per ball 4.5g total fat (2.8g saturated fat); 213kJ (51 cal); 0.2g carbohydrate; 2.6g protein; 0g fibre

radicchio with thai crab salad

PREPARATION TIME 20 MINUTES COOKING TIME 5 MINUTES (PLUS REFRIGERATION TIME) MAKES 64

¼ cup (60ml) water
¼ cup (60ml) lime juice
2 tablespoons white sugar
1 fresh red thai chilli,
chopped finely
500g fresh crab meat
1 lebanese cucumber (130g),
seeded, chopped finely
1 small red capsicum (150g),
chopped finely
2 green onions, sliced thinly
6 radicchio

1 Combine the water, juice, sugar and chilli in small saucepan; stir over low heat, without boiling, until sugar dissolves. Bring to a boil; remove from heat, cool. Cover; refrigerate dressing until cold.

2 Combine crab, cucumber, capsicum, onion and dressing in medium bowl.

3 Trim ends from radicchio; separate leaves (you need 64 leaves). Place 1 heaped teaspoon of the crab salad on each leaf. Serve cold.

tips We used radicchio, but you also can use red or green witlof, if you prefer. Dressing can be made a day ahead. Cover; refrigerate until required. Crab salad can be assembled up to four hours ahead. Cover; refrigerate until required.

per leaf 0.1g total fat (0g saturated fat); 42kJ (10 cal); 0.9g carbohydrate; 1.3g protein; 0.4g fibre

caramelised garlic and blue cheese tartlets

PREPARATION TIME 25 MINUTES **COOKING TIME** 40 MINUTES **MAKES** 24

20g butter

1 tablespoon olive oil

8 cloves garlic, peeled,
halved lengthways

1 large leek (500g), sliced thinly

2 teaspoons brown sugar

1 sheet ready-rolled puff pastry

60g blue cheese, crumbled

1 Heat butter and oil in large frying pan; add garlic, cook, stirring, over very low heat, about 10 minutes or until soft and browned lightly. Remove from pan.

2 Add leek to same pan; cook, stirring, until soft. Add sugar; cook, stirring occasionally, about 15 minutes or until mixture caramelises.

3 Preheat oven to hot (220°C/200°C fan-forced).

4 Cut rounds from pastry sheet using 4.5cm cutter. Place rounds on greased oven tray. Grease underside of another oven tray; place greased side on top of pastry (this cooks pastry through while stopping it from rising). Bake rounds in hot oven about 10 minutes or until browned lightly. Remove top oven tray.

5 Divide cheese among pastry rounds; top with caramelised leek and piece of garlic. Return tarts to oven for further 5 minutes or until cheese is soft. Serve warm.

tips Pastry rounds can be made a day ahead; the garlic and leek mixture can be made up to eight hours ahead. Top pastry rounds and reheat just before serving.

per tartlet 3.9g total fat (1.9g saturated fat); 222kJ (53 cal); 3.3g carbohydrate; 1.2g protein; 0.6g fibre

thai chicken salad in crispy wonton cups

PREPARATION TIME 40 MINUTES **COOKING TIME** 20 MINUTES (PLUS COOLING TIME) **MAKES** 40

2 cups (500ml) water
2 cups (500ml) chicken stock
2 chicken breast fillets (340g)
40 wonton wrappers
cooking-oil spray
¼ small chinese cabbage (175g), shredded finely
1 small carrot (70g), grated finely
3 green onions, sliced thinly
2 tablespoons toasted sesame seeds

DRESSING
⅓ cup (80ml) peanut oil
1 tablespoon white vinegar
1 tablespoon brown sugar
1 tablespoon soy sauce
1 teaspoon sesame oil
1 clove garlic, crushed

1 Combine the water and stock in medium frying pan; bring to a boil. Add chicken; return to a boil. Reduce heat; simmer, covered, about 10 minutes or until cooked through. Drain chicken; stand 10 minutes, chop finely.
2 Meanwhile, make dressing.
3 Preheat oven to moderately hot (200°C/180°C fan-forced). Lightly oil four 12-hole mini (1½ tablespoons/30ml) muffin pans.
4 Using 7.5cm-round cutter, cut one round from each wonton wrapper. Push rounds carefully into holes of prepared pans; spray lightly with oil.
5 Bake, uncovered, in moderately hot oven about 7 minutes or until wonton cups are golden brown. Stand in pans 2 minutes; turn onto wire racks to cool.
6 Meanwhile, combine chicken in large bowl with cabbage, carrot, onion, seeds and dressing.
7 Divide chicken salad among wonton cups, pressing down gently to fill. Serve immediately.

DRESSING Combine ingredients in screw-top jar; shake well.

tips Wonton cups can be made up to two days ahead. Keep in an airtight container. Chicken mixture can be prepared and refrigerated, covered, up to three hours ahead.
You need four 12-hole mini (1½ tablespoons/30ml) muffin pans for this recipe. If you do not own that many, make the wonton cups in batches, placing the cooked ones on a wire rack while you bake the remainder.

per cup 3.2g total fat (0.6g saturated fat); 234kJ (56 cal); 4.1g carbohydrate; 2.9g protein; 0.2g fibre

peanut and chicken gow gees

PREPARATION TIME 30 MINUTES (PLUS STANDING TIME) **COOKING TIME** 5 MINUTES **MAKES** 40

3 dried shiitake mushrooms

1 trimmed celery stalk (100g), chopped finely

1 tablespoon finely chopped, unsalted, roasted peanuts

1 clove garlic, crushed

1 green onion, chopped finely

2 teaspoons hoisin sauce

200g chicken mince

40 gow gee wrappers

DIPPING SAUCE

¼ cup (60ml) kecap manis

2 teaspoons red wine vinegar

1 Place mushrooms in small heatproof bowl, cover with boiling water; stand 20 minutes, drain. Discard stems; chop caps finely.

2 Meanwhile, make dipping sauce.

3 Combine mushrooms in medium bowl with celery, nuts, garlic, onion, sauce and chicken.

4 Place one heaped teaspoon of the chicken mixture in centre of one wrapper; brush around half of the wrapper's edge with a little water. Pleat damp side of wrapper only; pinch both sides together to seal. Repeat with remaining chicken mixture and wrappers.

5 Poach gow gees, in batches, in large saucepan of boiling water, or steam in bamboo steamer, about 5 minutes, until cooked through. Serve hot with dipping sauce.

DIPPING SAUCE Combine ingredients in small bowl.

tip Uncooked gow gees can be prepared up to four hours ahead. Cover; refrigerate until required.

per gow gee 0.7g total fat (0.2g saturated fat); 151kJ (36 cal); 5.4g carbohydrate; 1.1g protein; 0.2g fibre
per tablespoon dipping sauce 0g total fat (0g saturated fat); 29kJ (7 cal); 0.5g carbohydrate; 1g protein; 0g fibre

cocktails

piña colada

PREPARATION TIME 5 MINUTES

SERVES 1

45ml Bacardi
120ml bottled pineapple juice
30ml coconut cream
15ml Malibu
15ml sugar syrup
1 cup ice cubes

1 Blend ingredients on high speed until smooth.
2 Pour into a 400ml tulip-shaped glass. Garnish with two pineapple leaves and two straws.

per serving 6.3g total fat (5.5g saturated fat); 1120kJ (268 cal); 21.5g carbohydrate; 1g protein; 0.5g fibre

frozen strawberry margarita

PREPARATION TIME 5 MINUTES

SERVES 1

30ml tequila
15ml Cointreau
15ml strawberry liqueur
30ml fresh lime juice
4 frozen strawberries
1 cup ice cubes

1 Blend ingredients on high speed until smooth.
2 Pour mixture into a salt-rimmed 150ml margarita glass. Garnish with a strawberry wedge.

per serving 0.2g total fat (0g saturated fat); 798kJ (191 cal); 15.3g carbohydrate; 1.3g protein; 1.4g fibre

sugar syrup

PREPARATION TIME 1 MINUTE **COOKING TIME** 10 MINUTES **MAKES** APPROXIMATELY 1½ CUPS

Combine 1 cup (220g) white sugar and 1 cup (250ml) water in small saucepan; stir over low heat until sugar dissolves. Bring to a boil, then reduce heat and simmer, uncovered, without stirring, 5 minutes; remove from heat, cool. Store in an airtight container in the refrigerator for up to two months.

caipiroska

PREPARATION TIME 5 MINUTES

SERVES 1

1 lime, cut into 8 wedges
1 tablespoon grated palm sugar
60ml vodka
10ml sugar syrup
½ cup ice cubes
½ cup crushed ice

1 Using a mortar and pestle (or muddler), crush
   6 lime wedges with the sugar.
2 Combine lime mixture in cocktail shaker with
   vodka, sugar syrup and ice cubes.
3 Shake vigorously; pour into a 180ml old-fashioned
   tumbler with crushed ice; do not strain. Garnish
   with remaining lime wedges and two straws.

tip Palm sugar can be replaced with brown sugar.

per serving 0.2g total fat (0g saturated fat); 861kJ
(206 cal); 18.3g carbohydrate; 0.7g protein; 1.6g fibre

long island iced tea

PREPARATION TIME 5 MINUTES

SERVES 1

1 cup ice cubes
30ml vodka
30ml tequila
30ml Bacardi
30ml gin
15ml Cointreau
15ml fresh lemon juice
15ml sugar syrup
30ml cola

1 Place ice in glass; add vodka, tequila, Bacardi,
   gin and Cointreau.
2 Add juice and syrup, top with cola; stir.
3 Serve in a 300ml highball glass. Garnish with
   a twist of lemon rind, mint leaves and a straw.

per serving 0.1g total fat (0g saturated fat); 1488kJ
(356 cal); 18g carbohydrate; 0.1g protein; 0g fibre

duck broth with noodles

PREPARATION TIME 30 MINUTES **COOKING TIME** 30 MINUTES **SERVES** 6

1 chinese barbecued duck

3 cups (750ml) chicken stock

1.5 litres (6 cups) water

2 star anise

1 cinnamon stick

1 clove garlic, crushed

5cm piece fresh ginger (25g), sliced thinly

150g dried rice stick noodles

1 teaspoon sesame oil

200g gai larn, chopped coarsely

2 green onions, sliced thinly

¼ cup firmly packed fresh coriander

1 Remove meat and skin from duck. Remove and discard excess fat from meat and skin; reserve half the skin. Slice duck meat thinly.

2 Roughly chop duck bones and place in large saucepan with stock, the water, star anise, cinnamon, garlic and ginger. Bring to a boil; boil, uncovered, for 20 minutes. Strain liquid into another saucepan; return liquid to a boil.

3 Place noodles in medium heatproof bowl, cover with boiling water, stand for 5 minutes or until just tender; drain.

4 Add duck, sesame oil, half of the gai larn, half of the onion and half of the coriander to the broth; stir until hot.

5 To serve, divide noodles among bowls; top with broth, remaining gai larn, onion and coriander, then top with finely sliced reserved duck skin.

tips The stock mixture can be made a day ahead; complete soup just before serving.

Chinese barbecued duck can be purchased from Asian-food stores.

per serving 16.4g total fat (4.8g saturated fat); 1283kJ (307 cal); 17.7g carbohydrate; 22.2g protein; 2g fibre

soy and chilli squid

PREPARATION TIME 20 MINUTES (PLUS REFRIGERATION TIME) **COOKING TIME** 10 MINUTES (PLUS COOLING TIME) **SERVES** 6

500g squid hoods

12cm piece fresh ginger (60g).
sliced thinly

6 green onions, sliced thinly

2 fresh medium red chillies.
sliced thinly

⅓ cup (80ml) peanut oil

½ cup (125ml) light soy sauce

¼ cup (60ml) kecap manis

1 tablespoon sesame oil

1 Cut squid down centre to open out, score inside in diagonal pattern; cut into 5cm squares. Set aside in small bowl.

2 Combine ginger, half the onion and one of the chillies in small heatproof bowl. Heat peanut oil in small saucepan until moderately hot; carefully pour hot oil over ingredients in bowl. Slowly add sauce, kecap manis and sesame oil, whisking constantly; cool.

3 Pour two-thirds of the soy mixture over squid; cover, refrigerate 3 hours or overnight. Cover and refrigerate remaining soy mixture.

4 Drain marinade from squid. Cook squid, in batches, on heated, oiled barbecue plate (or grill or frying pan) until cooked through.

5 Toss squid with remaining onion and remaining chilli; serve with the remaining soy mixture.

tip This recipe can be prepared a day ahead. Cook just before serving.

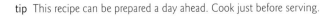

per serving 16.3g total fat (3g saturated fat); 911kJ (218 cal); 1.9g carbohydrate; 15.9g protein; 0.5g fibre

oysters with leek confit and salmon roe

PREPARATION TIME 30 MINUTES (PLUS STANDING TIME) **COOKING TIME** 45 MINUTES **SERVES** 4

3 small leeks (600g), sliced thinly
2 teaspoons salt
24 oysters on the half shell (600g)
50g butter
¼ cup (60ml) water
2 tablespoons salmon roe

1 Combine leek and salt in sieve over medium bowl; stand 1 hour.
2 Meanwhile, remove oysters from shells; wash shells, dry thoroughly, reserve. Refrigerate oysters until required.
3 Rinse leek under cold water; drain. Pat dry with absorbent paper.
4 Melt butter in medium frying pan, add leek and the water; cook, uncovered, stirring occasionally, over low heat about 45 minutes or until leek breaks down and is almost pulpy. Cool 10 minutes.
5 Divide shells among serving plates; divide leek confit among shells. Place one oyster on leek mixture; top with roe.

tip Salmon roe, also referred to as red caviar, makes a wonderful hors d'oeuvre. Sold fresh, it is extremely perishable and should be consumed in about three days. Always keep, covered, in the refrigerator.
Confit is a meat or vegetable that is preserved by salting and cooking slowly in fat, in this case, butter.

per serving 12.8g total fat (7.5g saturated fat); 723kJ (173 cal); 4g carbohydrate; 11g protein; 2.7g fibre

smoked salmon and mascarpone crepe cake

PREPARATION TIME 30 MINUTES (PLUS STANDING AND REFRIGERATION TIME) **COOKING TIME** 30 MINUTES **SERVES** 12

¾ cup (110g) plain flour

3 eggs

1 tablespoon vegetable oil

1⅓ cups (330ml) milk

2 cups (500g) mascarpone

2 tablespoons prepared horseradish

2 tablespoons drained capers, rinsed, chopped coarsely

2 tablespoons finely chopped fresh tarragon

1 tablespoon finely grated lemon rind

500g sliced smoked salmon

MIXED PEA SALAD

300g sugar snap peas, trimmed

200g snow peas, trimmed

150g snow pea tendrils

2 tablespoons olive oil

2 tablespoons lemon juice

1 Line base and side of deep 22cm-round cake pan with plastic wrap.

2 Place flour in medium bowl. Make well in centre; gradually whisk in combined eggs, oil and milk. Strain batter into large jug, cover; stand 30 minutes.

3 Heat oiled 22cm non-stick frying pan; pour about ¼ cup of the batter into pan, tilting pan so batter coats base evenly. Cook crepe, over low heat, loosening around edge with spatula, until browned lightly. Turn crepe; brown other side. Remove from pan; repeat with remaining batter to make a total of eight crepes.

4 Combine mascarpone, horseradish, capers, tarragon and rind in medium bowl. Place one crepe in prepared cake pan; spread with about ⅓ cup of the mascarpone mixture, cover with slices of salmon. Continue layering with remaining crepes, mascarpone mixture and salmon, finishing with crepe layer. Cover; refrigerate 3 hours or until firm.

5 Meanwhile, make mixed pea salad.

6 Cut crepe cake into 12 wedges; serve with mixed pea salad.

MIXED PEA SALAD Boil, steam or microwave sugar snap peas and snow peas, separately, until just tender; drain. Rinse under cold water; drain. Place in large bowl with remaining ingredients; toss gently to combine.

tips To make it easier to turn crepes, we used a heavy-based shallow non-stick frying pan.
If the mascarpone is too soft, the crepe cake's refrigeration time may need to be increased.
Crepes can be made up to two days ahead; wrap in plastic wrap and refrigerate until required. Crepe cake can be assembled the day before; store, covered, in refrigerator.

per serving 33.1g total fat (17.9g saturated fat); 1739kJ (416 cal); 14.3g carbohydrate; 16.3g protein; 2.2g fibre

cauliflower soup with cheese and bacon toasts

PREPARATION TIME 20 MINUTES COOKING TIME 20 MINUTES SERVES 6

1 tablespoon olive oil

1 medium brown onion (150g), chopped coarsely

2 cloves garlic, crushed

1 large potato (300g), chopped finely

1kg cauliflower, trimmed, chopped coarsely

3 cups (750ml) salt-reduced chicken stock

3 cups (750ml) water

2 tablespoons coarsely chopped fresh chives

CHEESE AND BACON TOASTS

3 thin bacon rashers (210g), quartered

1 thin crusty Italian-style bread

1 tablespoon wholegrain mustard

120g thinly sliced cheddar cheese

1 Heat oil in large saucepan; cook onion and garlic over low heat, stirring, until soft, but not coloured.

2 Add potato, cauliflower, stock and the water, bring to a boil. Reduce heat; simmer, covered, about 15 minutes or until vegetables are very soft.

3 Meanwhile, make cheese and bacon toasts.

4 Blend or process cauliflower mixture, in batches, until smooth; return to pan, stir gently over low heat until hot.

5 Divide soup among serving bowls; sprinkle with chives. Serve with cheese and bacon toasts.

CHEESE AND BACON TOASTS Place bacon on foil-covered oven tray; grill until browned and crisp. Slice bread diagonally into 12 thin slices. Grill bread slices until browned lightly; spread with mustard, top with cheese. Grill until cheese melts; top with bacon.

tips The soup can be made two days ahead.
The bacon toasts are best made close to serving.

per serving 14.3g total fat (6g saturated fat); 1404kJ (336 cal); 33.1g carbohydrate; 18.5g protein; 5.3g fibre

chilli quail, mandarin and grape salad

PREPARATION TIME 40 MINUTES (PLUS REFRIGERATION TIME) **COOKING TIME** 20 MINUTES **SERVES** 4

8 whole quails (1.6kg)

4 fresh small red thai chillies,
chopped coarsely

2 cloves garlic, halved

¼ cup (60ml) olive oil

2 tablespoons lemon juice

4 medium mandarins (800g)

300g snow peas, trimmed, halved

340g watercress, trimmed

1 cup (160g) toasted
blanched almonds

200g seedless red grapes,
halved lengthways

1 Using kitchen scissors, cut along both sides of each quail's backbone; discard backbones. Place each quail flat, skin-side down, on chopping board; cut and discard ribcages. Cut each quail into quarters.

2 Blend or process chilli, garlic, oil and half of the lemon juice until smooth; combine with quail pieces in large bowl. Cover; refrigerate 20 minutes.

3 Meanwhile, segment peeled mandarins over large bowl to save juice. Reserve segments and juice.

4 Cook undrained quail on heated, oiled grill plate (or grill or barbecue) until browned and cooked through.

5 Meanwhile, boil, steam or microwave peas until just tender; drain.

6 Place quail and peas in large bowl with mandarin segments and juice, watercress, nuts, grapes and remaining lemon juice; toss gently.

tips You can also cook the quail in a moderately hot oven for about 15 minutes, if you prefer.
Boned quails can be pre-ordered from your butcher or local poultry shop.

per serving 58.7g total fat (9.1g saturated fat); 3457kJ (827 cal); 25g carbohydrate; 50.8g protein; 10.5g fibre

asian-spiced roasted pork belly

PREPARATION TIME 10 MINUTES (PLUS REFRIGERATION TIME) **COOKING TIME** 1 HOUR 25 MINUTES **SERVES** 6

1kg pork belly, skin on, boned

½ cup (125ml) chinese
cooking wine

¼ cup (60ml) soy sauce

1 tablespoon tamarind concentrate

2 tablespoons honey

½ teaspoon sesame oil

4cm piece fresh ginger (20g),
chopped finely

3 cloves garlic, crushed

2 teaspoons five-spice powder

1 star anise

1 dried long red chilli

1 teaspoon sichuan pepper

3 cups (750ml) water

900g baby bok choy,
halved lengthways

1 Place pork in large saucepan of boiling water; return to a boil. Reduce heat; simmer, uncovered, about 40 minutes or until pork is cooked through, drain.

2 Meanwhile, combine wine, sauce, tamarind, honey, oil, ginger, garlic, five-spice, star anise, chilli, pepper and the water in large bowl, add pork; toss pork to coat in marinade. Cover; refrigerate 3 hours or overnight.

3 Preheat oven to hot (220°C/200°C fan-forced).

4 Place pork, skin-side up, on wire rack in large shallow baking dish; reserve marinade. Pour enough water into baking dish to come halfway up side of dish. Roast pork, uncovered, in hot oven about 30 minutes or until browned.

5 Meanwhile, strain marinade into small saucepan; bring to a boil. Boil, uncovered, about 20 minutes or until sauce reduces to about 1 cup.

6 Boil, steam or microwave bok choy until just tender; drain. Serve pork with sauce and bok choy.

tip Serve with steamed jasmine rice, if desired.

per serving 37.9g total fat (12.7g saturated fat); 2165kJ (518 cal); 10.1g carbohydrate; 32.6g protein; 2.3g fibre

vegetable pithiviers with roasted tomato sauce

PREPARATION TIME 45 MINUTES **COOKING TIME** 2 HOURS 5 MINUTES **SERVES** 4

10 large egg tomatoes (900g), quartered

2 teaspoons brown sugar

⅓ cup (80ml) olive oil

2 tablespoons red wine vinegar

2 large red capsicums (700g), halved

30g butter

2 large zucchini (300g), sliced thinly

7 flat mushrooms (560g), sliced thinly

1 clove garlic, crushed

1 tablespoon port

5 sheets ready-rolled puff pastry

1 egg yolk

1 tablespoon milk

50g baby spinach leaves

1 Preheat oven to moderate (180°C/160°C fan-forced).

2 Combine tomato, sugar, half of the oil and half of the vinegar in large bowl; place tomato pieces on oven tray. Roast, uncovered, in moderate oven 1 hour 40 minutes. Remove from oven; return to same bowl; crush with potato masher. Cover to keep warm.

3 While tomato is roasting, place capsicum, skin-side up, on oven tray. Roast, uncovered, in moderate oven about 40 minutes or until softened. Place capsicum in plastic bag; close tightly, cool. Discard skin, membrane and seeds; slice thinly.

4 Meanwhile, melt butter in large frying pan; cook zucchini, stirring, about 5 minutes or until softened. Place zucchini in small bowl; cover to keep warm. Place mushroom and garlic in same pan; cook, stirring, about 5 minutes or until mushroom softened. Add port; cook, stirring, until liquid evaporates.

5 Cut four of the pastry sheets into 16cm squares; cut remaining sheet into quarters. Place one of the small squares on oiled oven tray; centre a 9cm round cutter on pastry. Layer a quarter of the mushroom mixture, a quarter of the zucchini and a quarter of the capsicum on pastry; remove cutter. Brush border with combined egg yolk and milk; top with one of the large squares, press edges together to seal.

6 Using sharp knife, cut around pithiviers, leaving 5mm border; mark pastry with swirl design from centre to side, taking care not to cut through pastry. Brush lightly with egg mixture. Repeat process with remaining pastry, vegetables and egg mixture. Bake, uncovered, in moderate oven about 25 minutes or until pastry is browned lightly.

7 Meanwhile, combine spinach, remaining oil and remaining vinegar in medium bowl; toss gently. Divide salad among serving plates; serve with pithivier and roasted tomato sauce.

per serving 74.3g total fat (32.6g saturated fat); 4728kJ (1131 cal); 91.6g carbohydrate; 23.3g protein; 12.5g fibre

char-grilled veal with tomato, capers and basil

PREPARATION TIME 15 MINUTES **COOKING TIME** 20 MINUTES **SERVES** 6

9 baby eggplants (540g),
halved lengthways

6 small zucchini (540g),
sliced thickly

⅓ cup (80ml) extra virgin olive oil

6 veal cutlets (1kg)

2 medium egg tomatoes (150g),
seeded, chopped finely

½ small red onion (50g),
chopped finely

1 clove garlic, crushed

2 tablespoons drained small capers

1 tablespoon balsamic vinegar

1 tablespoon fresh baby basil leaves

1 Brush eggplant and zucchini with half of the oil; cook, in batches, on heated grill plate (or grill or barbecue) until browned and tender. Transfer to a plate; cover to keep warm.

2 Cook veal on heated, oiled grill plate (or grill or barbecue) until browned and cooked as desired. Transfer to a plate, cover veal; stand 10 minutes.

3 Meanwhile, combine tomato, onion, garlic, capers, vinegar and remaining oil in small bowl.

4 Divide eggplant and zucchini among plates; top with cutlets and tomato mixture, sprinkle with basil leaves.

tip Antipasto eggplant and zucchini may be used instead of fresh for a quicker alternative.

per serving 16.7g total fat (2.9g saturated fat); 1162kJ (278 cal); 3.6g carbohydrate; 28.2g protein; 2.7g fibre

deep-fried perch with chilli lime dressing

PREPARATION TIME 15 MINUTES **COOKING TIME** 20 MINUTES **SERVES** 4

3 lebanese cucumbers (390g)

3 medium carrots (360g)

4 small whole ocean perch (1.6kg), cleaned

vegetable oil, for deep-frying

½ cup (75g) plain flour

2 teaspoons salt

2 teaspoons ground white pepper

CHILLI LIME DRESSING

⅓ cup (80ml) sweet chilli sauce

2 teaspoons fish sauce

¼ cup (60ml) lime juice

1 teaspoon sesame oil

2 tablespoons coarsely chopped fresh thai basil

2 tablespoons coarsely chopped fresh vietnamese mint

2 tablespoons water

1 Using vegetable peeler, slice cucumbers and carrots lengthways into thin
   strips; combine in medium bowl.
2 Discard fish heads; score each fish three times on both sides.
3 Meanwhile, make chilli lime dressing.
4 Heat vegetable oil in wok. Combine flour, salt and pepper in medium shallow
   bowl; coat fish in flour mixture. Deep-fry fish, in two batches, until browned
   lightly and cooked through; drain on absorbent paper.
5 Divide carrot mixture among plates; top with fish, drizzle with chilli lime dressing.

CHILLI LIME DRESSING Place ingredients in screw-top jar; shake well.

per serving 15.2g total fat (2g saturated fat); 1647kJ (394 cal);
23.9g carbohydrate; 39.4g protein; 5.4g fibre

grilled herb polenta with semi-dried tomato and olive salad

PREPARATION TIME 15 MINUTES COOKING TIME 30 MINUTES (PLUS REFRIGERATION TIME) SERVES 4

2 cups (500ml) water

2 cups (500ml) vegetable stock

1 cup (170g) polenta

⅓ cup (25g) finely grated parmesan cheese

1 tablespoon finely chopped fresh flat-leaf parsley

1 tablespoon finely chopped fresh basil

SEMI-DRIED TOMATO
AND OLIVE SALAD

100g baby cos lettuce, trimmed, leaves torn roughly

1⅓ cups (200g) drained semi-dried tomatoes

4 green onions, sliced thinly

¼ cup (50g) thinly sliced pitted black olives

SPICED MAYONNAISE

¾ cup (225g) mayonnaise

pinch of cayenne pepper

¼ teaspoon ground cumin

¼ teaspoon ground coriander

¼ teaspoon ground turmeric

1 tablespoon lemon juice

1 Combine the water and stock in medium saucepan; bring to a boil. Gradually add polenta to liquid, stirring constantly. Reduce heat; cook, stirring, about 10 minutes or until polenta thickens. Stir in cheese, parsley and basil.

2 Spread polenta evenly into deep 19cm-square cake pan; cool 10 minutes. Cover; refrigerate about 3 hours or until firm.

3 Turn polenta onto board; trim edges. Cut into four squares, cut each square diagonally into two triangles. Cook polenta, in batches, on heated, oiled grill plate (or grill or barbecue) until browned both sides.

4 Meanwhile, make semi-dried tomato and olive salad. Make spiced mayonnaise.

5 Divide polenta among serving plates; top with salad, drizzle with spiced mayonnaise mixture.

SEMI-DRIED TOMATO AND OLIVE SALAD Combine ingredients in medium bowl.

SPICED MAYONNAISE Whisk ingredients in small bowl.

per serving 25.7g total fat (4.2g saturated fat); 2257kJ (540 cal); 62.4g carbohydrate; 13.8g protein; 9.6g fibre

slow-roasted duck with
sour cherry, apple and walnut salad

PREPARATION TIME 40 MINUTES **COOKING TIME** 2 HOURS **SERVES** 4

680g jar morello cherries

½ cup (125ml) chicken stock

½ cup (125ml) port

1 cinnamon stick

3 whole cloves

1 clove garlic, crushed

4 duck marylands (1.2kg),
excess fat removed

2 small green apples (260g)

1 cup (100g) toasted walnuts,
chopped coarsely

3 green onions, sliced thinly

1 cup firmly packed fresh
flat-leaf parsley leaves

2 tablespoons olive oil

1 tablespoon lemon juice

1 Preheat oven to moderately slow (160°C/140°C fan-forced).
2 Strain cherries over small bowl. Combine cherry juice with stock, port, cinnamon, cloves and garlic in large baking dish. Place duck on metal rack over baking dish; cover tightly with oiled foil. Roast, covered, in moderately slow oven about 2 hours or until duck is tender. Strain cherry sauce into large jug; skim away fat.
3 Cut apples into thin slices; cut slices into matchstick-sized pieces. Place apple and pitted cherries in large bowl with nuts, onion, parsley, oil and lemon juice; toss gently. Serve duck with salad and cherry sauce.

tip Do not slice apples until you're ready to assemble the salad as they will discolour.

per serving 81.2g total fat (18.8g saturated fat); 3963kJ (948 cal); 25.6g carbohydrate; 24.5g protein; 4.4g fibre

braised spatchcock with peas and lettuce

PREPARATION TIME 30 MINUTES **COOKING TIME** 1 HOUR **SERVES** 6

3 spatchcocks (1.5kg)

1 medium leek (350g)

2 bay leaves

1 sprig fresh thyme

1 sprig fresh rosemary

4 stalks fresh flat-leaf parsley

50g butter

2 cloves garlic, crushed

1 large brown onion (200g), chopped finely

8 bacon rashers (560g), rind removed, chopped coarsely

¼ cup (35g) plain flour

1½ cups (375ml) dry white wine

3 cups (750ml) chicken stock

1.5kg potatoes, chopped coarsely

¾ cup (180ml) milk

50g butter, extra

4 cups frozen peas (480g)

1 large butter lettuce, shredded finely

½ cup coarsely chopped fresh mint

1 Cut along both sides of spatchcocks' backbones; discard backbones. Cut spatchcocks in half between breasts; rinse halves under cold water, pat dry.

2 Cut leek in half crossways; chop white bottom half finely, reserve. Using kitchen string, tie green top half of leek, bay leaves, thyme, rosemary and parsley into a bundle.

3 Heat butter in large saucepan; cook spatchcock, in batches, until browned lightly both sides. Cook reserved chopped leek, garlic, onion and bacon in same pan, stirring, about 10 minutes or until onion softens. Add flour; cook, stirring, 2 minutes. Gradually add wine and stock; bring to a boil, stirring constantly, until mixture boils and thickens. Return spatchcock to pan with herb bundle, reduce heat; simmer, covered, 30 minutes.

4 Meanwhile, boil, steam or microwave potato until tender; drain. Mash potato with warmed milk and extra butter in large bowl until smooth. Cover to keep warm.

5 Discard herb bundle. Add peas, lettuce and mint to pan; simmer, uncovered, about 5 minutes or until peas are just tender.

6 Divide mashed potato among serving plates; top with spatchcock mixture.

tip Chicken pieces, quails or pigeons can be used rather than spatchcocks, if desired.

per serving 37.8g total fat (16.8g saturated fat); 3131kJ (749 cal); 44.9g carbohydrate; 47g protein; 11.3g fibre

lamb backstrap with vegetable crisps and beurre blanc

PREPARATION TIME 20 MINUTES **COOKING TIME** 35 MINUTES **SERVES** 4

½ small kumara (125g)
1 small parsnip (120g)
1 large beetroot (200g), trimmed
1 tablespoon olive oil
4 lamb backstraps (800g)
vegetable oil, for deep-frying

BEURRE BLANC
¼ cup (60ml) dry white wine
1 tablespoon lemon juice
¼ cup (60ml) cream
125g cold butter, chopped

1 Using vegetable peeler, slice kumara and parsnip into ribbons. Slice beetroot thinly.
2 Heat olive oil in large frying pan; cook lamb, in batches, about 5 minutes both sides or until cooked as desired. Cover to keep warm.
3 Make beurre blanc.
4 Heat vegetable oil in wok; deep-fry vegetables, in batches, until crisp. Drain on absorbent paper.
5 Cut each piece of lamb into three pieces. Divide half of the sauce among serving plates; top with lamb, remaining sauce and vegetable crisps.

BEURRE BLANC Combine wine and juice in medium saucepan; bring to a boil. Boil, without stirring, until reduced by two-thirds. Add cream; return to a boil. Whisk in cold butter, piece by piece, whisking between additions. Pour into medium jug; cover to keep warm.

per serving 48.4g total fat (25g saturated fat); 2805kJ (671 cal); 11.1g carbohydrate; 46.2g protein; 2.5g fibre

herbed and spiced sashimi with ginger cabbage salad

PREPARATION TIME 45 MINUTES COOKING TIME 5 MINUTES SERVES 4

2 tablespoons sesame seeds

1 tablespoon black sesame seeds

2 teaspoons coriander seeds

1 teaspoon sea salt

½ teaspoon cracked black pepper

2 tablespoons finely chopped
fresh chives

300g piece sashimi tuna

300g piece sashimi salmon

200g green beans, trimmed,
sliced thinly

6 trimmed red radishes (90g)

3 cups (240g) finely shredded
chinese cabbage

6 green onions, sliced thinly

1½ cups (150g) mung bean sprouts

1 cup firmly packed fresh
coriander leaves

GINGER DRESSING

2cm piece fresh ginger (10g), grated

2 tablespoons rice vinegar

2 tablespoons vegetable oil

2 teaspoons sesame oil

1 tablespoon mirin

1 tablespoon soy sauce

1 Dry-fry seeds in heated small frying pan, stirring, until fragrant; cool. Using mortar and pestle, crush seeds; combine in large bowl with salt, pepper and chives.

2 Cut each piece of fish into three 5cm-thick pieces. Roll each piece in seed mixture; wrap tightly, individually, in plastic wrap. Refrigerate until required.

3 Make ginger dressing.

4 Boil, steam or microwave beans until just tender; drain. Rinse beans under cold water; drain. Slice radishes thinly; cut slices into matchstick-sized pieces.

5 Combine beans and radish in large bowl with cabbage, onion, sprouts, coriander leaves and half of the dressing.

6 Unwrap fish; slice thinly. Divide fish and salad among serving plates; drizzle fish with remaining dressing.

GINGER DRESSING Combine ingredients in screw-top jar; shake well.

tips Salmon and tuna sold as sashimi have to meet stringent guidelines regarding their handling and treatment after leaving the water; however, it is best to seek local advice from knowledgeable authorities before eating any raw fish.
You need half a medium chinese cabbage for this recipe.

per serving 26.8g total fat (5.1g saturated fat); 1731kJ (414 cal); 3.6g carbohydrate; 39.3g protein; 5.2g fibre

cassoulet

PREPARATION TIME 40 MINUTES (PLUS STANDING TIME) **COOKING TIME** 2 HOURS 10 MINUTES **SERVES** 6

1½ cups (300g) dried white beans

300g boned pork belly, rind removed, sliced thinly

150g piece streaky bacon, rind removed, diced into 1cm pieces

800g piece boned lamb shoulder, cut into 3cm pieces

1 large brown onion (200g), chopped finely

1 small leek (200g), sliced thinly

2 cloves garlic, crushed

3 sprigs fresh thyme

400g can crushed tomatoes

2 bay leaves

1 cup (250ml) water

1 cup (250ml) chicken stock

2 cups (140g) stale breadcrumbs

⅓ cup coarsely chopped fresh flat-leaf parsley

1 Place beans in medium bowl, cover with water; soak overnight, drain.
  Rinse under cold water; drain. Place beans in medium saucepan of
  boiling water; bring to a boil. Reduce heat; simmer, covered, about
  15 minutes or until beans are just tender. Drain.
2 Preheat oven to moderately slow (160°C/140°C fan-forced).
3 Cook pork in large flameproof casserole dish over heat, pressing down
  with back of spoon on pork until browned all over; remove from dish.
  Cook bacon in same pan, stirring, until crisp; remove from dish. Cook
  lamb, in batches, in same pan, until browned all over.
4 Cook onion, leek and garlic in same dish, stirring, until onion softens. Add
  thyme, undrained tomatoes, bay leaves, the water, stock, beans and meat;
  bring to a boil. Cover; cook in moderately slow oven 45 minutes. Remove
  from oven; sprinkle with combined breadcrumbs and parsley. Return to oven;
  cook, uncovered, about 45 minutes or until liquid is nearly absorbed and
  beans are tender.

per serving 28g total fat (10.7g saturated fat); 2646kJ (633 cal);
39.5g carbohydrate; 54.9g protein; 12.1g fibre

slow-roasted lamb shanks with tomato and olives

PREPARATION TIME 15 MINUTES **COOKING TIME** 2 HOURS 25 MINUTES **SERVES** 4

8 french-trimmed lamb shanks (2kg)
¼ cup (35g) plain flour
1 tablespoon olive oil
1 clove garlic, crushed
¾ cup (180ml) dry white wine
¾ cup (180ml) salt-reduced beef stock
2 x 400g cans chopped tomatoes
6 anchovy fillets, drained, chopped coarsely
½ teaspoon dried chilli flakes
1 sprig fresh basil
1 cup (150g) pitted kalamata olives
1 tablespoon balsamic vinegar
½ cup loosely packed small fresh basil leaves, extra

1 Preheat oven to moderate (180°C/160°C fan-forced).

2 Toss lamb in flour; shake away excess flour. Heat oil in 3-litre (12-cup) flameproof casserole or baking dish; cook lamb, in batches, until browned all over.

3 Add garlic and wine to same dish; bring to a boil. Add stock, undrained tomatoes, anchovies, chilli and basil sprig; stir to combine.

4 Return lamb to dish; bring to a boil. Remove from heat. Cover with lid or tightly with foil; cook in moderate oven about 2 hours or until lamb is tender, turning lamb halfway through cooking. Remove lamb from dish; cover to keep warm.

5 Add olives and vinegar to dish; simmer, uncovered, over medium heat about 5 minutes or until thickened slightly. Remove basil sprig.

6 Sprinkle extra basil leaves over lamb and sauce; serve with risoni, if desired.

per serving 25.4g total fat (9.9g saturated fat); 2178kJ (521 cal); 16.8g carbohydrate; 48.6g protein; 2.3g fibre

gourmet chocolate tart

PREPARATION TIME 40 MINUTES (PLUS REFRIGERATION TIME) **COOKING TIME** 30 MINUTES **SERVES** 8

2 eggs
2 egg yolks
¼ cup (55g) caster sugar
250g dark eating chocolate, melted
200g butter, melted

TART SHELL
1½ cups (225g) plain flour
½ cup (110g) caster sugar
140g cold butter, chopped
1 egg, beaten lightly

1 Make tart shell.

2 Reduce oven to moderate (180°C/160°C fan-forced).

3 Whisk egg, egg yolks and sugar in medium heatproof bowl over medium saucepan of simmering water about 15 minutes or until light and fluffy. Gently whisk chocolate and butter into egg mixture.

4 Pour mixture into tart shell. Bake, uncovered, in moderate oven about 10 minutes or until filling is set; cool 10 minutes. Refrigerate 1 hour. Serve dusted with sifted cocoa powder, if desired.

TART SHELL Blend or process flour, sugar and butter until crumbly; add egg, process until ingredients just come together. Knead dough on floured surface until smooth. Enclose in plastic wrap; refrigerate 30 minutes. Grease 24cm-round loose-based flan tin. Roll dough between sheets of baking paper until large enough to line prepared tin. Lift dough onto tin; press into side, trim edge, prick base all over with fork. Cover; refrigerate 30 minutes. Preheat oven to moderately hot (200°C/180°C fan-forced). Place tin on oven tray; cover dough with baking paper, fill with dried beans or rice. Bake, uncovered, in moderately hot oven 10 minutes. Remove paper and beans carefully from tin; bake, uncovered, in oven about 5 minutes or until tart shell browns lightly. Cool to room temperature.

per serving 48.1g total fat (32.7g saturated fat); 2897kJ (693 cal); 60.4g carbohydrate; 8g protein; 2.6g fibre

sparkling stone fruit and raspberry jelly

PREPARATION TIME 15 MINUTES (PLUS REFRIGERATION TIME) **COOKING TIME** 10 MINUTES **SERVES** 6

½ cup (110g) caster sugar

750ml sweet sparkling wine

1½ tablespoons gelatine

½ cup (125ml) water

2 tablespoons lemon juice

1 medium nectarine (170g),
sliced thinly

2 medium apricots (100g),
sliced thinly

1 medium plum (110g),
sliced thinly

200g raspberries

1 Stir sugar and 1 cup of the wine in medium saucepan over heat, without boiling, until sugar dissolves; bring to a boil. Reduce heat; simmer, uncovered, without stirring, 5 minutes.

2 Meanwhile, sprinkle gelatine over the water in small heatproof jug; stand jug in small saucepan of simmering water. Stir until gelatine dissolves. Stir gelatine mixture, remaining wine and juice into wine mixture.

3 Divide fruit among six 1-cup (250ml) serving glasses. Pour wine mixture over fruit. Cover; refrigerate until firm.

tips You can use canned stoned fruit for this recipe if fresh fruit is out of season.
It's best to make this recipe a day in advance.

per serving 0.2g total fat (0g saturated fat); 815kJ (195 cal);
25.8g carbohydrate; 3.7g protein; 3g fibre

pear tart tatin

PREPARATION TIME 20 MINUTES (PLUS REFRIGERATION TIME) **COOKING TIME** 1 HOUR 15 MINUTES **SERVES** 6

3 large firm pears (990g)
90g butter, chopped
½ cup (110g) firmly packed brown sugar
⅔ cup (160ml) cream
¼ cup (35g) toasted pecans, chopped coarsely

PASTRY
1¼ cups (185g) plain flour
⅓ cup (55g) icing sugar mixture
90g butter, chopped
1 egg yolk
1 tablespoon water

1 Peel and core pears; cut lengthways into quarters.
2 Melt butter with brown sugar in large frying pan. Add cream, stirring, until sugar dissolves; bring to a boil. Add pear; reduce heat, simmer, turning occasionally, about 45 minutes or until tender.
3 Meanwhile, make pastry.
4 Preheat oven to hot (220°C/200°C fan-forced). Place pear, round-side down, in deep 22cm-round cake pan; pour caramelised pan liquid over pear, sprinkle with nuts.
5 Roll pastry between sheets of baking paper until slightly larger than circumference of prepared pan. Remove top paper, turn pastry onto pears. Remove remaining paper; tuck pastry between pear quarters and side of pan.
6 Bake, uncovered, in hot oven about 25 minutes or until pastry is browned lightly. Cool 5 minutes; turn tart onto plate, serve with whipped cream, if desired.

PASTRY Blend or process flour, icing sugar and butter until mixture is crumbly. Add egg yolk and the water; process until ingredients just come together. Enclose in plastic wrap; refrigerate 30 minutes.

per serving 41.9g total fat (24.5g saturated fat); 2700kJ (646 cal); 65.4g carbohydrate; 5.4g protein; 3.8g fibre

mango bombe alaska

PREPARATION TIME 20 MINUTES (PLUS FREEZING TIME) **COOKING TIME** 3 MINUTES **SERVES** 6

2 litres mango ice-cream, softened

¼ cup (60ml) orange juice

2 tablespoons orange-flavoured liqueur

16cm-round unfilled packaged sponge cake

1 large mango (600g), sliced thinly

4 egg whites

1 cup (220g) caster sugar

1 Line 15cm 1.375-litre (5½-cup) pudding basin or bowl with plastic wrap, extending plastic 5cm over edge of basin.

2 Pack ice-cream into prepared basin, cover with foil; freeze about 2 hours or until firm.

3 Preheat oven to very hot (240°C/220°C fan-forced).

4 Combine juice and liqueur in small jug. Trim top of cake to flatten; split cake in half horizontally through centre. Place bottom layer of cake on oven tray; brush with half the juice mixture. Top with mango then remaining cake half; brush with remaining juice mixture.

5 Invert ice-cream from basin onto cake; working quickly, trim cake to exact size of ice-cream. Return to freezer.

6 Beat egg whites in small bowl with electric mixer until soft peaks form; gradually add sugar, beating until sugar dissolves between additions.

7 Remove bombe from freezer; spread meringue over to enclose bombe completely. Bake, uncovered, in very hot oven about 3 minutes or until browned lightly. Lift onto serving plate; serve immediately.

tips If mango ice-cream is unavailable, place canned drained mango slices and scoops of vanilla ice-cream alternately in the pudding basin.
You can use Cointreau, Grand Marnier, Curaçao or any other orange-flavoured liqueur in this recipe.

per serving 22.8g total fat (13.9g saturated fat); 3018kJ (722 cal); 117.5g carbohydrate; 14g protein; 1.8g fibre

dark chocolate and almond torte

PREPARATION TIME 20 MINUTES **COOKING TIME** 55 MINUTES (PLUS COOLING AND STANDING TIME) **SERVES** 14

160g dark eating chocolate, chopped coarsely

160g unsalted butter

5 eggs, separated

¾ cup (165g) caster sugar

1 cup (125g) almond meal

⅔ cup (50g) toasted flaked almonds, chopped coarsely

⅓ cup (35g) coarsely grated dark eating chocolate

1 cup (140g) vienna almonds

DARK CHOCOLATE GANACHE

125g dark eating chocolate, chopped coarsely

⅓ cup (80ml) thickened cream

1 Preheat oven to moderate (180°C/160°C fan-forced). Grease deep 22cm-round cake pan; line base and side with two layers of baking paper.

2 Stir chopped chocolate and butter in small saucepan over low heat until smooth; cool to room temperature.

3 Beat egg yolks and sugar in small bowl with electric mixer until thick and creamy. Transfer to large bowl; fold in chocolate mixture, almond meal, flaked almonds and grated chocolate.

4 Beat egg whites in clean small bowl with electric mixer until soft peaks form; fold into chocolate mixture, in two batches. Pour mixture into prepared pan; bake, uncovered, about 45 minutes. Stand cake in pan 15 minutes; turn cake, top-side up, onto wire rack to cool.

5 Meanwhile, make dark chocolate ganache.

6 Spread ganache over cake, decorate cake with vienna almonds; stand 30 minutes before serving.

DARK CHOCOLATE GANACHE Stir ingredients in small saucepan over low heat until smooth.

tip Vienna almonds are whole almonds coated in toffee and are available from selected supermarkets, nut shops and gourmet food and specialty confectionery stores.

per serving 30.7g total fat (12.8g saturated fat); 1751kJ (419 cal); 30.6g carbohydrate; 7.5g protein; 1.9g fibre

almond and raspberry frozen puddings

PREPARATION TIME 25 MINUTES (PLUS FREEZING TIME) **SERVES** 8

3 eggs

⅓ cup (75g) caster sugar

600ml thickened cream

1 teaspoon vanilla extract

1 tablespoon cherry-flavoured liqueur

⅓ cup (45g) vienna almonds, chopped coarsely

⅔ cup (70g) frozen raspberries

200g white eating chocolate, melted

fresh raspberries, for serving, optional

1 Beat eggs and sugar in small bowl with electric mixer about 5 minutes or until the mixture is very pale and fluffy. Transfer to large bowl.

2 Beat cream, extract and liqueur in clean small bowl with electric mixer until soft peaks form. Gently fold cream mixture into egg mixture along with nuts and frozen raspberries.

3 Divide mixture among eight ¾-cup (180ml) moulds. Cover; freeze overnight or until firm.

4 Wipe moulds with hot damp cloth; turn out onto plates. Spoon melted chocolate over top; serve with fresh raspberries, if desired.

tips This recipe can be made a week ahead.
We used kirsch in this recipe, but any cherry-flavoured liqueur may be used.

per serving 40.2g total fat (24.1g saturated fat); 2077kJ (497 cal); 28.2g carbohydrate; 6.8g protein; 0.8g fibre

coffee and pecan puddings with caramel sauce

PREPARATION TIME 15 MINUTES **COOKING TIME** 40 MINUTES **SERVES** 6

¾ cup (90g) coarsely chopped toasted pecans
300ml cream
1½ cups (330g) firmly packed brown sugar
100g cold butter, chopped
125g butter, softened
1 teaspoon vanilla extract
½ cup (110g) caster sugar
2 eggs
1 cup (150g) self-raising flour
¼ cup (35g) plain flour
¼ cup (60ml) milk
1 tablespoon finely ground espresso coffee

1 Preheat oven to moderate (180°C/160°C fan-forced). Grease six ¾-cup (180ml) metal moulds or ovenproof dishes; line bases with baking paper.

2 Divide nuts among moulds; place moulds on oven tray.

3 Stir cream, brown sugar and chopped butter in small saucepan over heat, without boiling, until sugar dissolves. Reduce heat; simmer, uncovered, without stirring, about 5 minutes or until mixture thickens slightly. Spoon 2 tablespoons of the sauce over nuts in each mould; reserve remaining sauce.

4 Beat softened butter, extract and caster sugar in small bowl with electric mixer until light and fluffy. Add eggs, one at a time, beating until just combined between additions. Stir in sifted flours, milk and coffee; divide mixture among moulds. Bake, uncovered, in moderate oven 30 minutes. Stand puddings 5 minutes before turning onto serving plates.

5 Reheat reserved sauce. Serve puddings with sauce.

tips The caramel sauce and puddings can be made several hours ahead and reheated before serving.
Serve with cream or ice-cream, if desired.

per serving 62.2g total fat (33.8g saturated fat); 3921kJ (938 cal); 91.3g carbohydrate; 8.3g protein; 2.5g fibre

coffee snaps

PREPARATION TIME 15 MINUTES COOKING TIME 10 MINUTES PER TRAY (PLUS COOLING TIME) MAKES 70

125g butter, softened

1¼ cups (275g) firmly packed brown sugar

3 teaspoons ground coffee

½ teaspoon vanilla extract

1 egg

¾ cup (110g) plain flour

¾ cup (110g) self-raising flour

70 coffee beans

1 Preheat oven to moderate (180°C/160°C fan-forced).

2 Beat butter, sugar, coffee and extract in small bowl with electric mixer until light and fluffy. Add egg; beat until just combined. Stir in sifted flours.

3 Roll rounded teaspoons of mixture into balls. Place 3cm apart on greased oven trays. Top each with a coffee bean. Bake in moderate oven about 10 minutes. Transfer to wire racks to cool.

tip Coffee snaps can be made a week ahead.

per snap 1.6g total fat (1g saturated fat); 163kJ (39 cal); 6.1g carbohydrate; 0.5g protein; 0.1g fibre

almond shortbread drops

PREPARATION TIME 15 MINUTES **COOKING TIME** 20 MINUTES (PLUS COOLING TIME) **MAKES** 12

60g butter, chopped
½ cup (75g) plain flour
1 tablespoon rice flour
2 tablespoons icing sugar mixture
12 blanched almonds

1 Preheat oven to moderately slow (160°C/140°C fan-forced).

2 Process butter, flours and icing sugar until mixture forms a ball. Knead gently on floured surface until smooth.

3 Roll 2 teaspoons of mixture into balls; place on greased oven tray about 3cm apart. Top each ball with an almond.

4 Bake in moderately slow oven about 20 minutes or until browned lightly. Cool on tray.

tip This recipe can be made a week ahead.

per drop 4.9g total fat (2.8g saturated fat); 326kJ (78 cal); 7.7g carbohydrate; 1g protein; 0.4g fibre

rich mocha fudge

PREPARATION TIME 20 MINUTES **COOKING TIME** 15 MINUTES (PLUS COOLING AND REFRIGERATION TIME) **MAKES** 30 PIECES

1 cup (220g) caster sugar
⅔ cup (160g) sour cream
2 tablespoons glucose syrup
250g dark cooking chocolate, finely chopped
100g packet white marshmallows, roughly chopped
2 tablespoons coffee-flavoured liqueur
2 tablespoons dry instant coffee
2 teaspoons boiling water
30 chocolate-coated coffee beans

1 Grease 8cm x 25cm bar cake pan; line base and two long sides with baking paper.
2 Combine sugar, sour cream and glucose in small saucepan; stir over low heat, without boiling, until sugar dissolves. Using pastry brush dipped in hot water, brush down side of pan to dissolve any sugar crystals; bring to a boil. Boil, uncovered, without stirring, about 10 minutes or until syrup reaches 155°C when measured on a candy thermometer.
3 Remove from heat; add chocolate and marshmallow, stir until melted. Stir in combined liqueur, coffee and the boiling water.
4 Spread mixture into prepared pan; cool. Cover; refrigerate until firm.
5 Cut into 30 small squares; top each with a chocolate-coated coffee bean.

tips The recipe can be made up to four weeks ahead. Store, covered, in the refrigerator.
You can use a hazelnut-flavoured liqueur instead of the coffee-flavoured liqueur and top each piece with a halved hazelnut, if preferred.

per piece 4.9g total fat (3g saturated fat); 489kJ (117 cal); 18.3g carbohydrate; 0.8g protein; 0.2g fibre

pistachio bread

PREPARATION TIME 10 MINUTES **COOKING TIME** 45 MINUTES (PLUS COOLING AND STANDING TIME) **MAKES** 70 SLICES

3 egg whites
⅓ cup (75g) white sugar
¼ teaspoon ground cardamom
1 teaspoon finely grated orange rind
¾ cup (110g) plain flour
¾ cup (110g) shelled pistachios

1 Preheat oven to moderate (180°C/160°C fan-forced). Grease 8cm x 25cm bar cake pan; line base and sides with baking paper, extending paper 2cm above long sides of pan.

2 Beat egg whites in small bowl with electric mixer until soft peaks form. Gradually add sugar, beating after each addition until sugar dissolves; fold in cardamom, rind, flour and nuts. Spread bread mixture into prepared pan.

3 Bake in moderate oven about 30 minutes or until browned lightly; cool in pan. Wrap in foil; stand overnight.

4 Preheat oven to slow (140°C/120°C fan-forced).

5 Using a serrated knife, cut bread into 3mm diagonal slices. Place slices on ungreased oven trays. Bake in slow oven about 15 minutes or until dry and crisp; turn onto wire rack to cool.

tips Uncut bread can be frozen after the first baking. After the second baking, bread slices can be kept up to one week if stored in an airtight container.
For a different spiced version, omit the cardamom and use ½ teaspoon ground cinnamon and ¼ teaspoon ground nutmeg instead.

per slice 0.8g total fat (0.1g saturated fat); 81kJ (19.4 cal);
2.5g carbohydrate; 0.6g protein; 0.2g fibre

white chocolate snowball truffles

PREPARATION TIME 40 MINUTES COOKING TIME 5 MINUTES (PLUS REFRIGERATION TIME) MAKES 30

¼ cup (60ml) cream

30g butter

250g white chocolate Melts, chopped finely

½ cup (70g) slivered almonds, toasted

1 tablespoon almond liqueur

250g white chocolate Melts, melted, extra

1 cup (90g) desiccated coconut

1 Heat cream and butter in small saucepan; bring to a boil. Place chopped chocolate in medium heatproof bowl; add cream mixture, stir until smooth.

2 Stir in the almonds and liqueur. Cover and refrigerate, stirring occasionally, for about 30 minutes or until mixture begins to thicken. Roll rounded teaspoons of the mixture into balls; place in a single layer on plastic-lined tray. Refrigerate until firm.

3 Dip truffles into melted chocolate; gently shake off excess chocolate. Roll wet truffles in coconut; return to tray. Refrigerate until firm.

tip Truffles can be made two weeks ahead. Store in an airtight container in the refrigerator.

per truffle 6.3g total fat (3.9g saturated fat); 347kJ (83 cal); 5.8g carbohydrate; 1.1g protein; 0.4g fibre

glossary

bacon rashers also known as bacon slices.

beans
broad also known as fava, windsor and horse beans; available dried, fresh, canned and frozen. Fresh and frozen are best peeled twice, discarding both the outer long green pod and the tough beige-green inner shell.
butter cans labelled butter beans are, in fact, cannellini beans. Confusingly, butter is also another name for lima beans.
green sometimes called french or string beans,
kidney medium-sized red bean, slightly floury yet sweet in flavour; sold dried or canned.

beetroot also known as red beets.

bicarbonate of soda also known as baking soda.

bok choy also known as bak choy, pak choi, chinese white cabbage or chinese chard. Has a fresh, mild mustard taste; use stems and leaves. *Baby bock choy* also known as pak kat farang and shanghai bok choy, is smaller and more tender than bok choy.

breadcrumbs
packaged fine-textured, crunchy, purchased, white breadcrumbs.
stale one- or two-day-old bread made into crumbs by grating, blending or processing.

broccolini a cross between broccoli and chinese kale, is milder and sweeter than broccoli. From floret to stem, broccolini is completely edible.

butter use salted or unsalted (sweet) butter; 125g is equal to 1 stick butter.

cabanossi a ready-to-eat sausage; also known as cabana.

capsicum also known as bell pepper or, simply, pepper. Discard seeds and membranes before use.

cayenne pepper a thin-fleshed, long, extremely hot dried red chilli, usually purchased ground.

cheese
blue mould-treated cheeses mottled with blue veining.
bocconcini walnut-sized baby mozzarella, a delicate, semi-soft, white cheese. Spoils rapidly so must be kept under refrigeration, in brine, for one or two days at most.
cheddar most common cow-milk 'tasty' cheese; should be aged, hard and have a pronounced bite.
cream cheese commonly known as Philadelphia or Philly, a soft cow-milk cheese.
farm varies in texture, can be mild and sliceable or dry and crumbly.
fetta a crumbly textured goat- or sheep-milk cheese with a sharp, salty taste.
gruyere a swiss cheese having small holes and a nutty, slightly salty flavour.
haloumi a firm, cream-coloured sheep-milk cheese matured in brine; somewhat like a salty fetta in flavour, haloumi can be grilled or fried, briefly, without breaking down.

mascarpone a cultured cream product. Has a whitish to creamy yellow colour, and a soft, creamy texture.
mozzarella a soft, spun-curd cheese. It has a low melting point and a wonderfully elastic texture when heated.
neufchâtel similar in flavour and appearance to cream cheese, but contains less fat.
parmesan a hard, grainy cow-milk cheese also known as parmigiano.
pizza a commercial blend of processed grated mozzarella, cheddar and parmesan.

chilli available in many different types and sizes. Use rubber gloves when seeding and chopping fresh chillies as they can burn your skin. Removing seeds and membranes lessens the heat level.
dried flakes deep-red dehydrated extremely fine slices and whole seeds.
jalapeño fairly hot green chillies. Available in brine bottled or fresh from specialty greengrocers.
thai red small, bright red, medium-hot chilli.
powder can be used as a substitute for fresh chillies in the proportion of ½ teaspoon ground chilli powder to 1 medium chopped fresh chilli.

chinese cabbage also known as peking or napa cabbage, wong bok or petsai. Elongated in shape with pale green, crinkly leaves.

chinese cooking wine made from rice, wheat, sugar and salt, with 13.5% alcohol; available from Asian-food stores. If not available, mirin or sherry can be substituted.

chorizo a sausage of Spanish origin, made of coarsely ground pork and highly seasoned with garlic and chillies.

choy sum also known as pakaukeo or flowering cabbage, a member of the bok choy family; easy to identify with its long stems, light green leaves and yellow flowers. Is eaten, stems and all.

cocoa powder also known as cocoa.

coconut
cream the first pressing from grated mature coconut flesh; available in cans and cartons.
desiccated unsweetened, dried, finely shredded coconut.
milk second pressing (less rich) from grated mature coconut flesh.

coriander also known as pak chee, cilantro or chinese parsley; bright-green-leafed herb with a pungent flavour.

cornflour also known as cornstarch; used as a thickening agent in cooking.

couscous a fine, grain-like cereal product made from semolina; originally from North Africa.

cream we used fresh cream in this book, unless otherwise stated, also known as pure cream or pouring cream; has no additives. Minimum fat content is 35%.

crème fraîche mature, fermented cream having a slightly tangy, nutty flavour and velvety texture. Minimum fat content is 35%.
double thickened cream not for whipping. Minimum fat content 54%.
sour a thick, commercially cultured, soured cream. Minimum fat content is 35%.
thickened whipping cream containing a thickener. Minimum fat content 35%.

cumin also known as zeera.

currants dried, tiny, almost black raisins.

custard
powder packaged vanilla pudding mixture; combine with milk to make pouring custard.
vanilla prepared pouring custard.

eggplant also known as aubergine.

eggs some recipes in this book call for raw or barely cooked eggs; exercise caution if there is a salmonella problem in your area.

five-spice powder a fragrant mixture of ground cinnamon, cloves, star anise, sichuan pepper and fennel seeds.

flour
plain an all-purpose flour, made from wheat.
rice made from finely ground white rice.
self-raising plain flour sifted with baking powder in the proportion of 1 cup flour to 2 teaspoons baking powder.
wholemeal self-raising wholewheat flour, with baking powder added.

french shallot also known as golden shallots or eschalots.

gai larn also known as chinese broccoli, kanah, gai lum and chinese kale.

gelatine we used powdered gelatine; also available in sheet form known as leaf gelatine.

ghee clarified butter; can be heated to a high temperature without burning.

glucose syrup also known as liquid glucose.

gow gee wrappers wonton wrappers, spring roll or egg pastry sheets can be substituted.

horseradish, prepared grated horseradish bottled in salt and vinegar; different from horseradish cream.

jam also known as preserve or conserve.

kaffir lime leaves also known as bai magrood; looks like two glossy dark green leaves joined end to end, forming a rounded hourglass shape. Sold fresh, dried or frozen, the dried leaves are less potent so double the number called for in a recipe if you substitute them for fresh leaves. A strip of fresh lime peel can be substituted for each kaffir lime leaf.

kumara Polynesian name of orange-fleshed sweet potato often confused with yam.

mince meat also known as ground meat.

mirin a Japanese, champagne-coloured cooking wine made expressly for cooking and should not be confused with sake.

mixed peel candied citrus peel.

mixed spice a blend of ground spices usually consisting of cinnamon, allspice and nutmeg.

mushrooms
button small, cultivated white mushrooms with a mild flavour.
flat large, flat mushrooms with a rich, earthy flavour, they are sometimes misnamed field mushrooms, which are wild mushrooms.
oyster also known as abalone; grey-white mushroom shaped like a fan.
portobello large, dark brown mushrooms with full-bodied flavour, ideal for filling or barbecuing.
shiitake when fresh are also known as chinese black, forest or golden oak mushrooms; have the earthiness and taste of wild mushrooms. When dried, they are known as donko or dried chinese mushrooms; rehydrate before use.

mustard
american mild and sweet in flavour.
black mustard seeds also known as brown mustard seeds.
dijon a pale brown, distinctively flavoured, fairly mild french mustard.
wholegrain also known as seeded.

noodles
dried rice stick dried noodles made from rice flour and water, available flat and wide or very thin. Soak in boiling water to soften.
egg also known as ba mee or yellow noodles; made from wheat flour and eggs, and sold fresh or dried. Range in size from very fine to wide, thick spaghetti-like pieces.
fresh rice also known as ho fun, khao pun, sen yau, pho or kway tiau. Can be purchased in various widths or large sheets. Chewy and pure white, they do not need pre-cooking before use.
hokkien also known as stir-fry noodles; fresh wheat flour noodles resembling thick, yellow-brown spaghetti. Rinse under hot water to remove starch and excess oil before use.

oil
cooking-oil spray we use a cholesterol-free cooking spray made from canola oil.
olive made from ripened olives. Extra virgin and virgin are the first and second press.
extra light and *light olive* oils are diluted, and refer to taste not fat levels.
peanut pressed from ground peanuts; most commonly used oil in Asian cooking because of its high smoke point (capacity to handle high heat without burning).
sesame made from roasted, crushed, white sesame seeds; a flavouring rather than a cooking medium.

vegetable any of a number of oils sourced from plants rather than animal fats.

onion
green also known as scallion or, incorrectly, shallot; an immature onion having a long, bright-green edible stalk.
red also known as spanish, red spanish or bermuda onion; a sweet-flavoured, large, purple-red onion.
spring has small white bulbs, long green leaves and narrow green-leafed tops.

pancetta cured pork belly; if unavailable, bacon can be substituted.

parsley, flat-leaf also known as continental or italian parsley.

patty-pan squash also known as crookneck or custard marrow pumpkins.

pearl barley barley that has had the husk discarded and has been hulled and polished, similarly to rice.

pine nuts also known as pignoli.

polenta also known as cornmeal.

prawns also known as shrimp.

prosciutto cured, air-dried (unsmoked) pressed ham.

raisins dried sweet grapes.

rice
arborio small, round grain rice well-suited to absorb a large amount of liquid; especially suitable for risottos.
jasmine fragrant long-grained rice; white rice can be substituted, but will not taste the same.

rice paper sheets made from rice paste that's been stamped into rounds and can be kept at room temperature. Dipped briefly in water, these rounds become pliable wrappers for food.

rocket also known as arugula, rugula and rucola. Baby rocket leaves are smaller and less peppery.

saffron stigma of a member of the crocus family, available in strands or ground form; imparts a yellow-orange colour to food once infused. Should be stored in the freezer.

sambal oelek also ulek or olek; a salty paste made from ground chillies and vinegar.

sauces
barbecue a spicy, tomato-based sauce used as a condiment.
fish made from pulverised, salted, fermented fish (most often anchovies); has a pungent smell and strong taste.
hoisin a thick, sweet and spicy chinese paste made from salted fermented soy beans, onions and garlic; used as a marinade or baste.
kecap manis a dark, thick sweet soy sauce used in most South-East Asian cuisines.
oyster Asian in origin, this rich, brown sauce is made from oysters and their brine.

soy also known as sieu, is made from fermented soy beans.
sweet chilli the comparatively mild, thin Thai sauce made from red chillies, sugar, garlic and vinegar; often used as a condiment.
tomato also known as ketchup or catsup.
worcestershire a thin, dark-brown spicy sauce used as a seasoning or condiment.

shrimp paste also known as kapi, trasi and blanchan; made of salted dried shrimp.

snow peas also called mange tout ('eat all').

spinach also known as english spinach and, incorrectly, silverbeet.

star anise a dried star-shaped pod whose seeds have an astringent aniseed flavour.

stock 1 cup (250ml) stock is the equivalent of 1 cup (250ml) water plus 1 crumbled stock cube (or 1 teaspoon stock powder).

sugar we used coarse, granulated table sugar, (crystal sugar), unless otherwise specified.
brown an extremely soft, fine granulated sugar retaining molasses for its characteristic colour and flavour.
caster also known as superfine or finely granulated table sugar.
icing sugar mixture also known as confectioners' sugar or powdered sugar.
palm also known as nam tan pip, jaggery, jawa or gula melaka; made from the sap of the sugar palm tree. Usually sold in rock-hard cakes; substitute it with brown sugar if unavailable.

sumac a purple-red, astringent ground spice; adds a tart, lemony flavour to dips and dressings and goes well with barbecued meat. Can be found in Middle-Eastern food stores. *Substitute*: ½ teaspoon lemon pepper + ⅛ teaspoon five-spice + ⅛ teaspoon all spice = ¾ teaspoon sumac.

tamarind concentrate (or paste) result of the distillation of tamarind juice into a condensed, thick and purple-black paste. It is ready to use, with no soaking or straining required.

tomato paste triple-concentrated tomato puree.

tortillas thin, round unleavened bread. Can be made from either corn or wheat flour.

turkish bread also known as pide.

turmeric also known as kamin.

vanilla extract obtained from vanilla beans infused in water.

water chestnuts resemble chestnut in appearance, hence the English name. They are small brown tubers with a crisp, white, nutty-tasting flesh.

wonton wrappers also known as wonton skins. Substitute with gow gee, egg or spring roll sheets.

yeast allow 2 teaspoons (7g) dry granulated yeast to each 15g fresh yeast.

zucchini also known as courgette.

index

facts and figures

Wherever you live, you'll be able to use our recipes with the help of these easy-to-follow conversions. While these conversions are approximate only, the difference between an exact and the approximate conversion of various liquid and dry measures is but minimal and will not affect your cooking results.

dry measures

metric	imperial
15g	1/2oz
30g	1oz
60g	2oz
90g	3oz
125g	4oz (1/4lb)
155g	5oz
185g	6oz
220g	7oz
250g	8oz (1/2lb)
280g	9oz
315g	10oz
345g	11oz
375g	12oz (3/4lb)
410g	13oz
440g	14oz
470g	15oz
500g	16oz (1lb)
750g	24oz (1 1/2lb)
1kg	32oz (2lb)

liquid measures

metric	imperial
30ml	1 fluid oz
60ml	2 fluid oz
100ml	3 fluid oz
125ml	4 fluid oz
150ml	5 fluid oz (1/4 pint/1 gill)
190ml	6 fluid oz
250ml	8 fluid oz
300ml	10 fluid oz (1/2 pint)
500ml	16 fluid oz
600ml	20 fluid oz (1 pint)
1000ml (1 litre)	1 3/4 pints

helpful measures

metric	imperial
3mm	1/8in
6mm	1/4in
1cm	1/2in
2cm	3/4in
2.5cm	1in
5cm	2in
6cm	2 1/2in
8cm	3in
10cm	4in
13cm	5in
15cm	6in
18cm	7in
20cm	8in
23cm	9in
25cm	10in
28cm	11in
30cm	12in (1ft)

measuring equipment

The difference between one country's measuring cups and another's is, at most, within a 2 or 3 teaspoon variance. (For the record, one Australian metric measuring cup holds approximately 250ml.) The most accurate way of measuring dry ingredients is to weigh them.

When measuring liquids, use a clear glass or plastic jug with the metric markings. (One Australian metric tablespoon holds 20ml; one Australian metric teaspoon holds 5ml.

Note: North America, NZ and the UK use 15ml tablespoons. All cup and spoon measurements are level.

We use large eggs having an average weight of 60g.

how to measure

When using graduated metric measuring cups, shake dry ingredients loosely into the appropriate cup.

Do not tap the cup on a bench or tightly pack the ingredients unless directed to do so. Level top of measuring cups and measuring spoons with a knife. When measuring liquids, place a clear glass or plastic jug with metric markings on a flat surface to check accuracy at eye level.

oven temperatures

These oven temperatures are only a guide for conventional ovens.
For fan-forced ovens, check the manufacturer's manual.

	°C (Celsius)	°F (Fahrenheit)	Gas Mark
Very slow	120	250	1/2
Slow	150	275 – 300	1 – 2
Moderately slow	160	325	3
Moderate	180	350 – 375	4 – 5
Moderately hot	200	400	6
Hot	220	425 – 450	7 – 8
Very hot	240	475	9

Senior editor Wendy Bryant
Designer Caryl Wiggins
Food editors Louise Patniotis, Cathie Lonnie
Special feature photographer Brett Stevens
Special feature stylists Stephanie Souvlis, Jessica Sly, Sarah O'Brien
Special feature food preparation Elizabeth Macri
Assistant home economist Sharon Reeve
Nutritional information Angela Muscat
Food director Pamela Clark

ACP Books
Editorial director Susan Tomnay
Creative director Hieu Chi Nguyen
Sales director Brian Cearnes
Marketing director Matt Dominello
Brand manager Renée Crea
Production manager Carol Currie
Chief executive officer John Alexander
Group publisher Pat Ingram
Publisher Sue Wannan
Editorial director (AWW) Deborah Thomas

Produced by ACP books, Sydney.
Printed by SNP Leefung, China.
Published by ACP Publishing Pty Limited, 54 Park St, Sydney;
GPO Box 4088, Sydney, NSW 1028. Ph: (02) 9282 8618 Fax: (02) 9267 9438.
www.acpbooks.com.au
acpbooks@acp.com.au
To order books phone 136 116.
Send recipe enquiries to reccipeenquiries@acp.com.au
RIGHTS ENQUIRIES
Laura Bamford, Director ACP Books.
lbamford@acplon.co.uk
Ph: +44 (207) 812 6526
AUSTRALIA: Distributed by Network Services,GPO Box 4088, Sydney, NSW 1028.
Ph: (02) 9282 8777 Fax: (02) 9264 3278.
UNITED KINGDOM: Distributed by Australian Consolidated Press (UK),
Moulton Park Business Centre, Red House Rd, Moulton Park, Northampton, NN3 6AQ
Ph: (01604) 497 531 Fax: (01604) 497 533 acpukltd@aol.com
CANADA: Distributed by Whitecap Books Ltd, 351 Lynn Ave,
North Vancouver, BC, V7J 2C4 Ph: (604) 980 9852 Fax: (604) 980 8197
customerservice@whitecap.ca www.whitecap.ca
NEW ZEALAND: Southern Publishers Group, 44 New North Rd,
Eden Terrace, Auckland. Ph: (64 9) 309 6930 Fax: (64 9) 309 6170 hub@spg.co.nz
SOUTH AFRICA: Distributed by PSD Promotions (Pty) Ltd, PO Box 1175, Isando, 1600,
Gauteng, Johannesburg, SA. Ph: (011) 392 6065
Fax (011) 392 6079 orders@psdprom.co.za

Clark, Pamela.
The Australian Women's Weekly Eating In
Includes index.
ISBN 1 86396 422 3.
1. Cookery. I. Title. II Title: Australian Women's Weekly

641.5
© ACP Publishing Pty Limited 2005
ABN 18 053 273 546

The publishers would like to thank the following for props used in photography:
Villeroy and Boch, Freedom, Plenty Homewares, Ikea, Crave Homewares.

Cover: Barbecued chicken with nam jim, page 120
Photographer: Alan Benson
Stylist: Marie-Hélène Clauzon
Back cover: White chocolate snowball truffles, page 240
Photographer: Brett Stevens
Stylist: Sarah O'Brien

Photographers: Alan Benson, Adrian Lander, Andre Martin, Ben Dearnley,
Brett Stevens, Chris Chen, Ian Wallace, Joe Filshie, Louise Lister, Prue Ruscoe,
Simon Furlong, Steve Brown, Stuart Scott, Tim Robinson
Stylists: Wendy Berecry, Julz Beresford, Janelle Bloom, Kate Brown, Kirsty Cassidy,
Marie-Hélène Clauzon, Georgina Dolling, Jane Hann, Amber Keller, Opel Khan,
Michelle Noerianto, Sarah O'Brien, Louise Pickford, Linda Venturoni-Wilson